POP★PEOPLE™

Ashlee Simpson

POP★PEOPLE™

Ashlee Simpson

by Louise Casapulla

SCHOLASTIC INC.

New York   Toronto   London   Auckland   Sydney   Mexico City   New Delhi   Hong Kong   Buenos Aires

ISBN: 0-439-76581-1

Copyright © 2004 Scholastic Inc.
All rights reserved. Published by Scholastic Inc.
POPPEOPLE is a trademark of Scholastic Inc.

12 11 10 9 8 7 6 5 4 3 2 1   5/0 6/0 7/0 8/0 9/0 10/0

Printed in the U.S.A.
First printing, April 2005

CONTENTS PAGE

INTRODUCTION

White-hot spotlights lit up the sky outside Hollywood's exclusive Concorde Club as the photographers surrounding the red carpet squirmed impatiently. Behind the police barricades, fans excitedly stood on tiptoes while a steady stream of plush SUVs and limousines lined up at the curb waiting to drop off their famous occupants. Car doors opened and party guests like Kelly Osbourne, actor Shane West, and all three members of the rock band Good Charlotte got out, smiled for the cameras and fans, and then slowly made their way inside.

But on this night, there was only one girl everyone was waiting for — Ashlee Simpson, dancer, actress, reality TV star, songwriter, and now, finally, a rock star! The party at the exclusive Hollywood club was being held to celebrate the release of her debut CD, *Autobiography*. But the night was more than just a party, it was the exact moment that Ashlee's lifelong dream came true.

Making an Entrance

Applause and shouts from her fans greeted Ashlee when she finally arrived on the scene with her parents, Tina and Joe Simpson, who smiled proudly as their youngest daughter posed for the cameras. "A father's dream is seeing his daughter's dream come true, and it happened this week," Joe Simpson told a reporter. Added Tina: "It is overwhelming! I am so proud of her and we are all so blessed. She is making her own shadows now. It took a lot for Ashlee to make this record and step outside of expectations."

For her big party, Ashlee had spent a lot of time deciding what she would wear. She'd finally chosen a hot-pink multilayered dress by designer Matthew Williamson that made her look pretty but, in keeping with her new rock star image, a little bit edgy too. With her toenails painted to match her hot-pink sandals and a cool, oversized silver watch designed by jeweler-to-the-stars Jacob the Jeweler dangling from her wrist, the teenager best known for her casual style suddenly appeared every bit the glamorous star. To complete her look for her big evening, Ashlee wore smoky eye makeup to emphasize her huge, blue-green eyes, clear supershiny lip gloss, and just a touch of glitter to light up her pretty face. Her long brown hair — which she'd changed from blond just a few months before — flowed gently down her back.

Ashlee had every reason to look and feel like a star. While her first single, "Pieces of Me," had gotten a lot of attention in the weeks leading up to the party, her debut album, *Autobiography*, had done even better. It was almost leaping from record stores and into the hands of her eager fans, topping the *Billboard* chart faster than anyone had expected.

"For me, my goal was to sell 80,000 the first week," Ashlee confessed to a reporter from a celebrity magazine. "The first day my album came out it hit 150,000. They said, 'Honey, by two o'clock in the afternoon you already passed 80,000.' I had no clue!"

Many of the friends that Ashlee made during her two seasons on *7th Heaven* had turned out to congratulate her on her big night. *American Dreams* star Brittany Snow arrived at the party with Tyler Hoechlin, who Ashlee had shared some screen kisses with when he played Martin on *7th Heaven*.

3

Brittany praised Ashlee for staying so normal, despite her new success. "The coolest thing about Ashlee is that she really doesn't care about fame," Brittany told a reporter. "We went shopping in the mall and she wore sweats and looked blah. Everyone was recognizing her but she was down-to-earth and natural."

ER actor Shane West, who starred with Mandy Moore in the teen romance *A Walk to Remember*, also described Ashlee as one cool girl. "I've known Ashlee for years," he confided. "She's a real sweetheart. She is very honest, very cool."

"She actually got me to dance once," he added sheepishly. "It happened at a party about a year ago. I'm not a dancer but it's hard to say no to her. The fact that it happened at a party made it even more embarrassing because there was a small amount of people there. It was very hard."

Throughout her life, Ashlee has had a way of getting what she wants, even if it hasn't come easily. She began dancing at the age of four, and by 11 years old she was accomplished enough to be accepted as a student at a prestigious New York ballet school. However, she eventually discovered that the dedicated life of a ballerina wasn't for her.

At 14, Ashlee moved with her family to California — though she still wasn't sure what she wanted to do with her life. Although she joined her sister, Jessica, onstage as a backup dancer, she also gave acting a try, landing the role of supersweet Cecilia Smith on *7th Heaven*, a recurring character for two seasons.

Still, Ashlee wanted more. To that end, she agreed to let MTV's cameras follow her around as she worked on her own album of music. *The Ashlee Simpson Show* became a hit. Viewers couldn't help but fall under the spell of Ashlee, a girl who was sweet, honest, and down-to-earth, even as she dreamed of becoming a rock star. Along the way, fans identified with Ashlee as she had her heart broken by her first boyfriend, Josh. They felt her pain as she tried to put her feelings into the lyrics of a song and struggled to get people to see her as more than the little sister of singer and reality TV darling Jessica Simpson, star of *Newlyweds*. It was impossible not to root for Ashlee as she fell for a new boy, singer Ryan Cabrera. By the time the series concluded, fans felt like Ashlee had become more than just a girl on TV; she had become their friend.

"Making my record has been like a journey," Ashlee explained to a reporter. "I feel like I've grown up so much. Going into the record I felt like everything was going so great. I had a boyfriend and life was just so dandy. But so much of everything in my life took a different turn — I got my heart broken and I learned a lot from that."

Lots of girls — and even a few boys — related to what Ashlee went through and they proved it by making the album that chronicled her heartbreak and her new love number one the very first week it was released. "I'm just very excited, overwhelmed, and extremely happy," Ashlee confessed to a reporter. "You pour your heart out when you make a record, and for people to react the way they do is so amazing."

As Ashlee gave a last wave to the reporters, photographers, and fans before entering the Concorde Club, she couldn't help feeling that she'd finally found her own special place in the world.

CHAPTER 1
Childhood Dreams

How many girls have seen *The Nutcracker* and dreamed of becoming a ballerina? Certainly too many to count! Every year, as the winter holidays approach, this classic ballet has a knack for casting a magic spell on girls who leave the theater asking their parents for their own pair of pink ballerina slippers and a pretty tutu in which to practice pirouettes.

Like so many young girls, Ashlee began her dreams of dancing across a stage in a beautiful costume very early in life. Tina and Joe's youngest daughter, who was born Ashlee Nicole Simpson in Waco, Texas, on October 3, 1984, began dancing at the age of four and fell in love with it immediately.

In fact, both Ashlee and sister Jessica, who is four years older, took classes in jazz dancing, ballet, tap, and hip-hop dancing from the time that they were very young. But while Jessica, who gave her first public performance singing "Amazing Grace" in church at age five, liked dancing, Ashlee loved it! Ashlee spent many hours twirling around the house or backyard, with her little dog Jordan (who Jessica named after New Kids on the Block's Jordan Knight) yapping at her feet.

In the Beginning

Ashlee was born into a creative family. Her father, Joe, who was also the youngest child in his family, wanted to be an actor when he was growing up in San Antonio, Texas. As a high school student, he won a statewide championship for his acting in the play *Cyrano de Bergerac* and attended Baylor University in Waco, Texas, on a drama scholarship. But when money became tight, he was force to leave school and find a job.

Joe became a youth minister in a Baptist church. The outgoing, handsome young man enjoyed working with kids and teaching them how to handle life's problems or leading missionary trips to work in soup kitchens or paint churches in Los Angeles and New York. "Not only was I a minister, but I was a thera-pist," Joe explained to *Billboard* magazine. "I spent my time healing relationships. I also spent my time teaching people to tell the truth." One person who was instantly captivated by Joe was a pretty blond named Tina.

Tina, who was 18 when she married Joe Simpson, also came from a musically gifted family. Tina's mother played violin and piano, and Ashlee explained in an interview, "My mom has an incredible voice. She never wanted to be a singer, but she was just blessed with a good voice."

After Joe and Tina married, they were blessed with two daughters they named Jessica Ann and Ashlee Nicole, and the young family settled in Richardson, Texas.

From their earliest days, the differences between Ashlee and Jessica were obvious. "Ashlee likes to test the waters more than Jessica," mom Tina told *People* magazine.

"One is comedy, the other is drama," Joe told the *New York Daily News*. Guess which one Ashlee is?

And it's true, while Jessica has always been the good, obedient daughter, Ashlee tended to be a little bit more experimental, more direct, and a tiny bit rebellious at times. "I would push the line," Ashlee explained to an interviewer. "I probably was the one who got in more trouble. But I always had a

9

conscience, so I would never do something I would feel guilty about because I knew I would have to live with it!"

While Jessica has a natural tendency to be shy, her little sister has always been the more outgoing and direct. "If I have a problem with somebody, I'll walk up and say something, but Jessica's always nice to people," Ashlee told a teen magazine. "I'm more like, 'Honey, you need to change.'"

While Jessica spent her early years cheerleading and singing with her church youth band, Ashlee set her sights on becoming a prima ballerina. At age 11, after years of dance lessons, Ashlee applied to take a summer session at the prestigious School of American Ballet in New York City.

Ballerina Dreams

Each summer, the School of American Ballet, which is affiliated with the world-famous New York City Ballet, accepts up to 200 young ballerinas, usually between the ages of 12 and 18, to train with some of the world's best dancers and choreographers. Ashlee became the youngest person ever to attend the school's summer session.

But the life of a ballerina isn't all bright lights and pretty costumes. It's extremely hard work, perhaps harder than any 11-year-old could expect. At the School of American Ballet, summer students spend hours perfecting their technique and honing their body's strength and stamina so they can eventually make the most difficult dance moves look effortless. At the end of each day, students would inevitably go back to their dorm rooms with aching muscles and stiff, swollen feet.

At the end of five weeks, Ashlee returned home from New York doubtful that she loved ballet enough to choose it as a career. "I got burned out on it," Ashlee told the *Chicago Tribune*. "I don't dance ballet at all anymore."

It's also very likely that this native Texas girl missed her hometown a lot that summer. After all, Ashlee admits that, even today, she still gets homesick sometimes. "I miss Texas so much," she said wistfully during a 2004 MSN chat. "I always say I can't wait to settle down and move to Austin."

Rockin' Out

Fortunately, giving up ballet wasn't the end of Ashlee's creative life. Around the same time that she came home from New York, she discovered the awesome power of rock music. "The first CD that I remember listening to was something that my cousin played for me, which was Van Halen," she told a teen magazine. "So I used to listen to their CDs and wear their T-shirts. My cousin wanted to make me a rocker."

Ashlee also discovered some popular music on her own. "Since I was like 11, I loved rock music," she recalled for a reporter. "I had orange hair, I was definitely listening to Green Day, and all that kind of stuff. I just liked that kind of music."

Imagine the arguments the Simpson sisters must have had over the stereo at home! For while Jessica was honing her vocal skills by listening to divas like Mariah Carey and Whitney Houston, Ashlee was rocking out to female rockers like Pat Benatar, Blondie's Deborah Harry, Fiona Apple, No Doubt's Gwen Stefani, and 60's legend Janis Joplin.

"I was probably like 11 years old when I went to the Lilith Fair," Ashlee told MTV. "I saw Jewel and Joan Osborne, and I was like, 'I want to be like them.'"

Eventually, Ashlee would be able to put all the lessons she learned from listening to those rock 'n' roll CDs — as well as some of the poise and grace she learned onstage at the School of American Ballet — to good use. But it wouldn't be for a little while yet.

CHAPTER 2
California, Here We Come!

In 1997, Ashlee's older sister, Jessica, signed a record deal with Columbia Records. For the whole Simpson family, it was a dream come true. But it also meant big changes for everyone. Tina and Joe strongly believed that families should never be separated, so it was decided that the entire family would move to Los Angeles, where Jessica was recording her album.

Ashlee, who was 13 at the time, couldn't help but be happy for Jessica. And although she was sad to leave her friends behind in Texas, she was thrilled to be moving to the star-making capital of the world. "I wrote on my dream list 'move to Los Angeles,'" Ashlee revealed in an interview. "Ever since I was really, really young I wanted to be an actress. So when my parents said, 'What do you think about going to L.A. and auditioning for stuff?' I was like, 'Oh my gosh.' It was like a dream come true for me."

To prepare for the move, Joe Simpson gave up his job as a youth counselor at the church and made plans to manage Jessica's and Ashlee's careers full-time. Though the idea of working with a parent might upset some kids, Ashlee was happy that she didn't have to share her dad's attention with the other children at the church anymore. "My dad was like a dad to a ton of other kids," Ashlee recalled to a reporter from the *New York Times*. "Now he focuses on us and he really looks out for our best interests."

"There's stories that Hollywood breaks up the family," added Joe during an interview with ABC's *20/20* news magazine. "In our case, I think it saved our family." In fact, all four members of the Simpson clan admit that they became closer after they started working together. That was particularly true of Ashlee and Jessica, who really bonded after the move to the Golden State. "We had left all our friends behind," Ashlee told a newspaper. "So we pretty much had no one else to hang out with!"

"People are always like, 'Oh, it's very weird that your parents hang out with you,' but it's not,"

Ashlee explained to the *New York Times*. "It's so great. I don't hide one thing from my parents."

Mom's New Role

Where did Ashlee's mother, Tina, fit in? Easy. As Jessica began meeting with record company people or doing promotions, Tina naturally fell into the role of wardrobe shopper, dresser, and even designer at times. "I love clothes — I just don't like to shop for them," Jessica confessed to a teen magazine in 2001. "I don't like to try clothes on. But my mom would always make them magically appear!"

Ashlee, who was starting to go out on auditions for television and commercial roles, also enjoyed the benefits of her mother's sense of style. "My mom is a hip lady," Ashlee told the *New York Times*. "She knows my style and she knows Jessica's style. I tend to put a lot of random things together, ever since I was a little kid. I'll wear cowboy boots and a leotard, or snow boots and a thing on my head and tights or whatever. Sometimes they don't match, and so my mom, sometimes she'll be like, 'maybe you should put some shoes on that match.' She'll make sense of something, and keep it my style, but make it more TV-friendly."

In the Shadows

Jessica's work in the recording studio on the album that would be her 1999 debut, *Sweet Kisses*, fascinated Ashlee, but she had her own mind set on becoming an actress. She worked hard to ignore the little voice in her head that kept suggesting that she should try singing too. It was a time in her life when Ashlee was very aware of being the younger sister to beautiful, talented Jessica, a person who everyone around them was saying would one day be a huge star. Ashlee loved and admired Jessica and her parents, but her adolescent feelings of being overlooked, neglected, and unloved were very real. They would eventually find their way into one of *Autobiography*'s most heartfelt songs, "Shadow."

"Jessica has always been the singer, but whatever Jessica sang, Ashlee would sing louder," Joe explained to a reporter. "But when Jessica really started rising, Ashlee pulled back and didn't want to be compared as a singer. In fact, we never heard her sing in public until she did her first show."

As a rebellious 14-year-old, Ashlee swore she would never follow in Jessica's footsteps and become a singer, even though deep down inside it was what she wanted more than anything in the world. "When I was younger, because my sister was a singer, I was not a singer," Ashlee told MTV.

"I was much more shy about singing," she told *In Touch*. "I would just sort of write in my room."

Putting aside her love of music, Ashlee set her sights on becoming an actress. While Jessica spent time in the recording studio with her dad, Tina would drive Ashlee to acting auditions after school. Ashlee also took acting classes from famed Los Angeles-based theater coach Janet Alhanti. The time Ashlee put into becoming the best actress paid off and she even won a few small jobs. "I did, like, a Kohl's commercial and a couple of other commercials like here and there," Ashlee explained to a magazine.

But Ashlee couldn't totally forget about music. Around this time, she first discovered Alanis Morissette, the former Canadian child star who became a worldwide sensation with the hit "You Oughta Know," in which the singer angrily tells the boy who broke her heart how much he hurt her. Unfortunately, Ashlee's mom was less than thrilled that Ashlee had discovered the song, because its lyrics contained naughty words she didn't think were appropriate for her teenage daughter to sing around the house. In fact, when Alanis's concert came to Los Angeles, Tina wouldn't allow Ashlee to go. "My mom wouldn't let me go see Alanis, which made me want to listen to her even more," Ashlee told a reporter from the *Los Angeles Times*.

In fact, Ashlee got quite rebellious. "I kept saying (a bad word) to make her mad," Ashlee recalled to the Associated Press with a giggle. "I got my mouth washed out with soap!"

Fortunately, Tina and Joe didn't freak out too much. In fact, years later, on the song "Shadow," Ashlee would thank her entire family for being so understanding of the confusing time she went through as a young teenager. "My parents really weren't that strict," Ashlee told AP. "They know I'd go off the wall if they were."

Fortunately, there was no need to go off the wall. Ashlee was about to receive an offer that would change her life forever.

CHAPTER 3
On the Road

Once Jessica's album on Columbia Records, *Sweet Kisses*, was released at the end of 1999, life in the Simpson house got very, very busy. In the beginning, Tina would stay home with Ashlee, while Jessica flew around the country with Joe to promote her first single, the sweet ballad "I Wanna Love You Forever." While Ashlee was going to high school and shopping at the mall, Jessica was signing autographs, performing onstage, and telling interviewers all about her life.

At times, Joe and Tina must have worried that splitting the family in half wasn't a good idea. There must have been times when Ashlee and Tina, sharing a lonely dinner in their California home, looked at the empty seats around their table sadly. Jessica and Joe must have been homesick a lot too.

After all, hotels and fancy dinners stop feeling so glamorous once you realize that you miss you own bed, friends, and the ability to spend the day doing anything you feel like.

But an answer to how the whole family could support Jessica's career and stay together was about to present itself. When "I Wanna Love You Forever" hit the Top 10, Jessica was offered her first national concert tour opening up for 98° on their "Heat It Up" tour at theaters and arenas around the country.

Of course, everyone knows this is the place where Jessica would grow close to her future husband, Nick Lachey, who was then the lead singer of 98°, but the tour also helped the Simpson family stay together. "Jessica came up to me and said, 'Ashlee, I really want you to come dance for me. Will you dance for me?'" Ashlee explained to an interviewer. "And so I got the opportunity to go dance with her for about three years."

It was the perfect solution. When Jessica would begin her concert tour, the whole family would go along: Joe as her manager, Tina as her wardrobe consultant, and Ashlee, then 14, as one of her backup dancers.

The Wanderers

By the time the tour started, Ashlee had already spent several weeks of rehearsal with Jessica, a choreographer, and the other dancers. Although Ashlee was once again the youngest person in the group, the dancers were all friendly and fun to be around. Years after leaving the ballet stage, Ashlee finally had her chance to shine. She found that her dance training was useful in helping her learn the choreography and get used to being in the right place at the exact moment the music began.

One of the most memorable moments in preparing for their very first tour was the first time that Ashlee and Jessica got a chance to explore their home away from home — the Simpson family tour bus. Because flying between concert dates would be too expensive, most performers travel on a tour bus, a vehicle that functions as a hotel room as well as a place to work, play, and get some much needed peace and quiet.

The girls were surprised by how nice the bus was — most are light-years away from the bumpy, rattling school buses many kids take to school. Tour buses are more like giant recreation rooms on wheels. There's a full-size refrigerator for snacks, a microwave oven, running water, a shower and toilet, and comfortable chairs and tables to sit and read a book or eat a meal. There are enough bunks aboard for everyone to get a good night's sleep — in fact, many performers say that they get so used to the rocking sensation of the moving bus that they miss it when they sleep in a real bed! Additionally, tour buses are built to keep people entertained on long drives, so they're always equipped with a TV area — usually with a satellite TV hookup — comfy couches, books, CDs, DVDs, and a console for video games.

Traveling Schoolhouse

For Ashlee, the tour bus would also become her classroom. Like her sister, Jessica, who received her high school degree through home study, Ashlee was tutored in all her high school classes — from English and math through history and biology — by her mom for a minimum of three hours each day.

"Every class that you go through in high school, my mom taught me," Ashlee told the *New York Times*. "When everyone else got to go play, I'd have to sit down and do work in the back of the bus!"

But it wasn't all bad because Ashlee's fellow

dancers liked to keep her company as she did her schoolwork. "My sister's dancers would come over and help me out if I needed to know something," Ashlee confided to a reporter from the *New York Times*. "Jessica had a Latin dancer, so I was going though Spanish classes and he would totally help me."

It took Ashlee two years, but by the time she reached her sweet 16 birthday, she passed the test to receive her high school diploma. Although her life on the road made her miss out on the normal things that go along with high school life — football games, parties, the prom, and graduation celebrations — she says that was okay. The experiences she had traveling around the country and spending time with her family more than made up for the things she missed out on.

"If I had to go back, I wouldn't change a thing," she told the *Chicago Tribune*. "I have a great life."

A Day in the Life

After a while, Ashlee got used to the pattern that most days on the road followed. If it was the day of a show at a new venue, the Simpson family tour bus would arrive early. Usually, as the road crew got the stage ready, there were a few hours of free time for Ashlee, where she'd catch up on her schoolwork or join the other dancers for some sightseeing or a pickup game of basketball. Although Jessica and her dad were usually busy with interviews and other promotional efforts on the first day in a new city, Ashlee could count on having her mom around to take her shopping at a nearby mall.

A few hours before Jessica's show was scheduled to begin, Ashlee, her family, all the dancers, and the road crew got together for a meal backstage at the venue. While the food was never as good as Mom's cooking, there'd usually be a couple of good choices, like chicken, pasta, salad, and inevitably something yummy and chocolate for dessert. Fortunately, Ashlee didn't have to worry too much if she had a piece of chocolate layer cake — dancing onstage every night kept all the dancers slim. "Doing shows is like the best exercise ever," Ashlee told an interviewer. "I run around and sweat like a madwoman. But that's what's so much fun about doing live shows. We are so into it. We are not into looking good, we are really into having fun."

It was also fun to be a part of the backstage community. After a while, Ashlee got to know the names of most of the crew. In the three years she spent on the road, she also became friendly with the members of the other acts who shared the bill with Jessica, like the members of 98°, Beyonce Knowles, Michelle Williams, and Kelly Roland of Destiny's Child, and the members of the Irish girl group B*witched.

Ashlee must have looked forward to that moment right before the show began when Jessica, the dancers, her parents, and anyone else who was backstage held hands and said a quick prayer for a good show and no injuries. As she stood in the dark, the anticipation of running onstage to the cheers and applause of the crowd was almost too much to bear. Ashlee loved it all — from the first second she joined Jessica through the complex dance routines she knew by heart to the inevitable moment when Jessica would introduce her to the audience as her little sister.

In a way, Ashlee was becoming known too. Fans started recognizing her. She even occasionally got fan mail — not as much as Jessica, naturally, but enough to make her proud.

In addition to appearing on the concert stage at every stop on Jessica's tour, Ashlee also had a chance to join her sister for some of her television appearances. Over the three years that Ashlee traveled with Jessica, she appeared alongside her sister on shows like *Saved by the Bell*, *The Donny & Marie Show*, *The Rosie O'Donnell Show*, *The View*, and *The Tonight Show with Jay Leno*. Ashlee also took the stage during Jessica's Disney Christmas concert special.

The three years that Ashlee spent on tour with Jessica were wonderful, unforgettable, and thrilling, but it still wasn't enough. For although Jessica was really fantastic about introducing Ashlee to everyone and taking her along on fun things like photo shoots, Jessica was still the star of the show.

Looking for something to call her own, Ashlee did her last tour with Jessica and returned home to California, where she planned to try acting again. "Being onstage is a rush, but right now, I'm leaning more towards acting," Ashlee told *Tiger Beat* magazine in 2001. "I really love doing it."

CHAPTER 4
Finding 7th Heaven

At 17, Ashlee was determined to make her way as an actress. She felt that the years she spent on the road with her sister had really helped her mature and develop the skills she'd need to convince a casting director that she was exactly the right person for the part. Armed with a photo — called a headshot in the entertainment industry — and the poise and confidence that she developed over the years, Ashlee started attending open calls and knocking on doors in hopes of receiving her big break.

Her television breakthrough came when she won a role on an episode of the Fox comedy *Malcolm in the Middle*. Though the part was small — so small that her character "high school girl" didn't have a real name, Ashlee was thrilled to be on the hit comedy and determined to make the most of the experience. Along the way, her outgoing personality and upbeat manner made her a lot of friends on the *Malcolm* set, including series star Frankie Muniz, who became a really close pal and a big fan of Ashlee's music.

In *7th Heaven*!

Ashlee's next big break came when she won the role of Cecilia, a classmate of Simon Camden, on the long-running WB family drama *7th Heaven*.

The popular series follows the adventures of the Camden family, a California minister, his wife, and their seven children as they share life, love, laughter, and the occasional heartbreak. Ashlee, who as the daughter of a former minister herself really identified with *7th Heaven*, was introduced in the seventh season as Cecilia, the love interest of actor David Gallagher's character, Simon. As Cecilia, Ashlee would get a chance to kiss both David and their costar Tyler Hoechlin, who joined the cast as Martin in the eighth season.

"They are both very good kissers," Ashlee confided during an MSN Internet chat. "It's never like a real kiss when you're doing on-screen kisses. David was my first on-screen kiss."

29

Kissing Tyler was even less romantic! "Tyler and I would joke around and eat pickles and Doritos to see who could get the worst breath!" Ashlee admitted on MSN.

For a while, Ashlee was very excited about her acting career and the opportunity to join the 7th *Heaven* cast as a regular member. The two years that she lived in California, often without seeing her sister for weeks at a time, was a confidence builder. "When I'm acting, the characters that I choose are people that have dignity and strength," she told MTV. "My character on 7th *Heaven,* she always stands up for herself, and I really like that."

As Cecilia, she earned her own paycheck and her own fans — fans who didn't just like her because she was Jessica Simpson's little sister. By the end of her run on 7th *Heaven*, Ashlee had more than 50 Internet sites devoted to her, and while that wasn't as many as her sister had, it still made her feel really good.

"Being on 7th *Heaven* was so cool and such an awesome experience," she recalled during an MSN chat. "I love the cast . . . and my fans are so awesome."

Ashlee also made her big-screen debut in 2002, playing the role of Monique in funnyman Rob

Schneider's hit comedy *The Hot Chick*. The movie also starred *Scary Movie*'s Anna Faris, Matthew Lawrence, and Tia and Tamara Mowry. One of Ashlee's favorite young female rockers, Michelle Branch, even made a cameo appearance in the film playing a DJ.

Music Dreams

As her success as an actress made Ashlee love herself more, that new confidence made her begin to think about getting back into music. Suddenly, she didn't feel quite the same need to distance herself from Jessica.

"When I was younger, because my sister was a singer, I was not a singer," she told MTV. "But I loved singing, so I was like, 'Why am I not doing this for myself?' I can't not do a record just because my sister has a record. I knew there was going to be a lot of flack for that, people are going to say, 'Oh my gosh, you're trying to be like your sister.' But I'm like, 'No, dude, a lot of people like music.'"

"I'm not going to *not* do music just because my sister sings," Ashlee added to the Associated Press. "The Jacksons did it. It runs in your genes."

But there are a lot of differences between

31

Jessica's heartfelt ballads and the kind of music that Ashlee wanted to do. "Our personalities are so different and it reflects in our music," Ashlee told AP.

Even as she continued to enjoy being a part of 7ᵗʰ *Heaven*, Ashlee couldn't stop herself from writing down lyrics in the notebook she often carried, or humming a tune to herself as she was sitting on the set in the makeup chair. She looked to other female rockers like Courtney Love and Gwen Stefani for inspiration. "Even when I got into 7ᵗʰ *Heaven*, I continued doing music," Ashlee told an interviewer.

But it wasn't always so easy. In 2001, Ashlee signed a recording contract with a new record label started by MTV personality Carson Daly. It seemed like a match made in heaven. As the host of *TRL* through the late nineties and into the new millennium, blue-eyed Carson was his generation's answer to *American Bandstand* host Dick Clark, interviewing everyone from Backstreet to Britney and Mariah to Madonna. To teenagers everywhere, Carson was the master of ceremonies who dictated who was cool and who wasn't.

But Ashlee's celebration was short-lived. By the end of the year, Carson's record label was no more and she was back to being an actress who dreamed of singing and was waiting for someone to come along and make her dreams come true.

Life's a Beach

But Ashlee's luck was about to turn around. In the summer of 2003, she got the opportunity to become a cohost at MTV's beach house in New York's posh Hamptons. But boy, was she in for a surprise! Although the MTV beach house, which that summer was located in East Quogue, New York, seems like it's always hosting one big party, filming shows like *TRL* and *MTV Hits* outside a television studio is a lot of work.

"I thought the beach house would be this great resort, this Club Med where they'd be partying 24/7," said Tom Tadlock, a beach house regular in the summer of 2003 to *Newsday*. "It's the first TV production that I've ever done in my life, so it was a big learning experience. When we got here, it was just one gigantic set with hundreds of crew members running around. This is no resort. This is all business."

And contrary to popular belief, no one lives at the MTV beach house, which meant that Ashlee and whichever parent was traveling with her spent most of the summer living at a local hotel. On days when she was working, Ashlee would show up at the beach house very early, have her hair and makeup done, and then chill out in one of the "green rooms." The green rooms were actually the beach house's bedrooms, which were turned into waiting rooms for the hosts like Ashlee and the different performers who'd come to play at the beach house.

When the weather was nice and everyone was outside on the deck, dancing to the latest song by Will Smith, the beach house was a great place to be. But when the weather was wet, rainy, and cold and everyone still had to pretend to have fun, Ashlee really put her skills as an actress to good use. "It's always something you have to deal with when you go outside," said Tony DiSanto, a senior vice president of MTV Productions. "We try to have fun with it."

By the end of the summer, Ashlee had gotten a lot of experience in front of a camera and it was great. Instead of playing Cecilia on *7th Heaven*, she was just being Ashlee Simpson. "With acting, people judge your character and how you portray it," Ashlee said to *Billboard* magazine. But going in front of the camera and playing yourself is an entirely different situation. "You're letting your guard down and opening yourself up in front of people," she said. "It's the real you."

Good-bye, Cecilia

By the end of the summer of 2003, Ashlee had one more reason to celebrate. A song she recorded, "Just Let Me Cry," was released on the *Freaky Friday* soundtrack. The album, which also featured singles from Lindsay Lohan (who starred in the movie), the Donnas, and Simple Plan, introduced Ashlee's music to tweens and teens everywhere.

And there was still more good news around the corner. Ashlee finally landed a contract with Geffen Records to record her own album of tunes!

It was finally the moment she'd been waiting for — time to rock out like she'd always dreamed. In preparation for the album to come, she wrote poems and potential lyrics to songs. "My inspiration came from what I have gone through in the past three years," she said during a chat on MSN. "Every single day, I was thinking of what I was going through and would write songs about it."

But as one door opens, another must close. So as Ashlee proceeded to work toward her music career, she had to bid the character she'd played for

35

two years good-bye. Knowing she wouldn't be returning for the ninth season of 7th Heaven, Ashlee bid farewell to Cecilia by changing her hair color.

"I dyed my hair brown on the day I finished 7th Heaven," she told a reporter. "I had the same haircut and blond hair for two seasons and I was over it."

Instead of going to a salon to make the big change, Ashlee impulsively decided to take matters into her own hands. "I went to Target with my best friend and I brought a maroon hair color and a brown one and a black one," she told a reporter.

Of course, making a drastic change — like going from very light hair to very dark — is always risky, and Ashlee worried about the results. "I had bottle-blond hair . . . and I'd had the same haircut forever for the show," she said in another interview. "So, I hoped it didn't turn green!"

Fortunately, it didn't. "When I came up from the sink, I was incredibly shocked," she told the *New York Times*. "But now I don't want to go blond again."

In fact, the first color Ashlee tried wasn't quite brunette enough. "I dyed it brown and then made it a little bit darker," she explained. "But I decided the maroon might be a little extreme."

Naturally, Ashlee was worried about what her parents would think. She decided to show Tina first. "I called my mom and said, 'Hey, I did something,'" Ashlee recalled in an interview. "I told her I did something to myself and I was going to come over and show it to her. She was like, 'Oh, Ash, you didn't get a tattoo?' and I said, 'Maybe!' I totally didn't, but when I went over, she loved my hair," Ashlee continued.

Changing her hair color from blond to brunette made Ashlee feel more mature and more confident. "I feel like I have come into my own a bit now," she explained in an interview. "It has changed my style. I think I looked really young with blond hair. I still look really young, but I feel like I can wear more skirts and things like that, where before I was more tomboyish. Now, I feel more womanly."

And this woman was ready to take on the world!

CHAPTER 5

The Ashlee Simpson Show

As 2004 dawned, Ashlee was preparing to record her debut album. Unlike a lot of young performers who end up singing songs written by other people, this Texas spitfire was determined to have a hand in writing the songs she would sing. "I wasn't going to make a record unless I could write on every song," she told *Billboard*. "It really makes a difference [when you're performing] to speak from your own experiences."

And what experiences! Over the next few months, every moment of Ashlee's life would become inspiration for her debut album. "I'm going through some defining moments in my life," she said. "I've tried not to hold anything back, but I guess I should apologize to all of the boys that I have used for inspiration."

A Bright Idea

But while Ashlee was going about the business of searching for inspiration and writing songs, her dad, who brokered her deal with Geffen Records, had the bright idea to create a new MTV show with Ashlee as its star. After all, a reality TV series on MTV had already done wonders for Jessica's career.

After the initial success of her debut album, *Sweet Kisses*, Jessica's career had hit a speed bump. Her 2001 sophomore effort, *Irresistible*, proved to be anything but irresistible to record buyers — it bombed!

But Jessica, who married her boyfriend, Nick Lachey, in October 2002, got a real career boost from their MTV series, *Newlyweds*. In fact, the show became so successful that Columbia Records put an extra big push behind her third album, *In This Skin*, to capitalize on her new popularity. It ended up going double platinum, selling some 2.4 million copies. For the first time ever, Jessica was the "it" girl, suddenly hotter than her old rivals Britney Spears and Christina Aguilera.

So Joe proposed to MTV and Ashlee that they make a new TV series about the recording of Ashlee's music. "The design for me, originally, was to have

39

each show focus on one song and why it was written," Joe explained to *Billboard* magazine. "Her series is *The O.C.* with music, because it's the drama of her life."

It was a brilliant idea, but there was one problem — Ashlee didn't want to do it. She had been around the MTV cameras as they followed Jessica and Nick to create *Newlyweds* and hated the idea of living her life under the watchful eyes of complete strangers. "I'd been around my sister's cameras and I was like, 'There is no way that I'm going to do a reality show,'" Ashlee recalled for *Entertainment Weekly*.

Plus, she still was wary about following too closely in Jessica's footsteps, worried that people would make the inevitable comparisons between the two. But her dad promised it wouldn't be like that. "I wasn't that wild about having the cameras in my face," Ashlee told the Associated Press. "But my dad thought it would be a good way for everyone to get to know me as me, and not as Jessica's little sister."

In the end, Ashlee relented and acknowledged the wisdom of her father's idea. But instead of filming a huge 13-episode season, as was done for *Newlyweds*, MTV created sort of a miniseries for Ashlee.

In the end, the cameras spent just nine hours a day, two days a week, following her.

"Nobody really knew that much about me," Ashlee told the *Chicago Tribune*. "This was my way of saying, 'Here's who I am.' I chose to just be myself and let it happen and have fun."

The "Unreachable" Boy

The first episode of the show focused on getting to know the major players in Ashlee's life: Ashlee; her mom, Tina; her dad, Joe; and her roommate, an old elementary school pal named Lauren Zelman, who had moved to Los Angeles to become an actress. As the gals moved to a brand-new apartment, Tina popped by to offer some advice on keeping the place neat. "I had to learn to clean and be on my own," Ashlee explained to *US*.

Of course, there were some early traumas, like Ashlee discovering that her new bedroom closet wasn't ideal. "My closet is definitely not big enough for all my stuff," she told a reporter. "I probably have 100 pairs of shoes, but I can usually only find one of each!"

In the first episode, viewers also got a chance to meet Ashlee's boyfriend of two years, Josh

Henderson, 22, who was also a singer. At first, Josh and Ashlee seemed like the perfect pair. They spent time cruising around in Ashlee's Lexus, bowling, going to parties, and joking around. But when Ashlee goes to write music and Josh is there, she's embarrassed because all her songs are about him.

Unfortunately, Ashlee and Josh's problems run even deeper. By the end of the episode, she's worried that she and Josh are "not on the same page." Her instincts are right. Although the cameras aren't there to see it, before the episode is over Josh breaks up with Ashlee and breaks her heart. "You always think you are going to marry the guy," Ashlee said of her first love, "and then you realize you're not."

"I learned that when you first lose your first love it's like, oh my God, it's like the end of the world," Ashlee told an interviewer. "But then you look back, finally, you're like, 'Ah, whatever.' But he was your first love and it happens to everybody."

But it took a long time for Ashlee to get over Josh. She recounted for a reporter from *Entertainment Weekly* how she felt when she ran into him at a Los Angeles nightspot and he pretended he barely knew her.

"I know this is dorky," Ashlee said, "but when he was leaving . . . I was really mad. Really mad.

He acted like he never met me before. I was like, 'Okay, I can't wait till you hear my album.' I learned that I don't want a boyfriend like him," she told an interviewer.

The hurt Ashlee felt over Josh had one good result — it gave her something to write about. In the end, the songs "Autobiography" and "Unreachable" off her debut album were about him. "Whenever I'm hurt, it's so much easier to let it out and write about it from a tough perspective," she told MTV.

Writing songs about Josh even helped her to heal and move on with her life. "My heart got broken for the first time from a guy," Ashlee explained to a reporter from the *New York Times*. "But now I have this perspective. I totally could be his friend now."

"Like, I got over him," she added to *Entertainment Weekly*. "Guys come and go, but you're the one that has to stay strong."

"It's not a big deal now, but I felt like it at that point," she added in a *New York Times* interview. "Now it's more of a reflection, a memory stored away, and now I love to date around and not be too serious, just be 19 and have fun."

The Bad Guy

In addition to teenage drama and heartache, the road to becoming a rock star can be really hard. Another episode of *The Ashlee Simpson Show* chronicled Ashlee's battles with Geffen Records president Jordan Schur.

Jordan was shown criticizing Ashlee's work and even saying at one point that he wanted her music to sound "nicer." Ashlee, for her part, became frustrated, afraid that her music would have more in common with Hilary Duff than Courtney Love. Not that Ashlee has anything personal against the former *Lizzie McGuire* star, she just doesn't care for her music. "I don't know how else to say it but that's just not me," Ashlee told the Associated Press. "I think it's great, but I'm just drawn to different stuff."

Jordan's other goal was making sure that Ashlee sounded nothing like her older sister, Jessica, an idea that rocker Ashlee agreed with from the start. "Ashlee told me coming in, 'I'm not my sister. I like rock,'" Jordan explained to *Entertainment Weekly*. "I knew there were times when she wouldn't understand me and would get angry — which she did — and I don't care about that. My job is to make a great record."

But the battles between Ashlee and the record company executive were sometimes traumatic, especially when her father, Joe, took the record company's side. "When I was arguing with Ashlee and I was firing her producers, and she was crying, 'Dad, I'm so upset, do something,' any other manager — forget father — would have jumped in," Jordan told *Billboard*. "Joe sat there and didn't open his mouth. He said, 'Listen to Jordan.'"

Meet the Parents

On the more positive side, *The Ashlee Simpson Show* also allowed viewers to get an inside look at Ashlee's relationships with both of her parents. Although she sometimes became angry with her father for business decisions she didn't agree with, it was easy to see how much love existed between Ashlee and Joe. "My dad and I, we'll, like, go head-to-head and fight," Ashlee told MTV. "I have to admit it, and sometimes I don't want to, but I think that I'm him!

"Me and my dad are very strong-minded and what we say is how we feel and we're not going left or right of it," Ashlee continued. "But two seconds later after a fight, I'm like, 'Daddy, I love you! I'm so

45

sorry!' Because we love each other at the end of the day, and I know even if I want to fight him for something, I know that he's not out to get me."

The relationship between Ashlee and her mom, Tina, was even easier to understand. Unlike a lot of moms and daughters who never agree, this pair really enjoys spending time together and usually sees eye-to-eye on most topics. "My mom is my best friend in the whole world," Ashlee proudly told MTV.

Tina, a stay-at-home mom who taught aerobic classes in her spare time, was instrumental in making her girls the positive, independent women they have become. "My mom has really taught us to be ourselves and individual people, which is very cool," Ashlee explained to MTV. "If I want my hair to be orange, she can go, 'Oh God, don't dye your hair orange,' but she lets me express myself however I want. So if I was to get a tattoo, I think that she probably wouldn't love it, but she knows that it's me and I'm gonna do what I wanna do."

When she stops to think about it, Ashlee admits that she owes her mom a world of thanks. "I think my mom raised me and Jessica very free and open and not really feeling like we had anything to hide," she told an interviewer.

In fact, despite Ashlee's rebellious streak, she and her mother rarely get into disagreements that they can't figure out. "My mom is incredible," Ashlee told the *New York Times*. "I always listen to her."

Well, maybe not always! Ashlee admitted that there have been a few minor disagreements between them. "We're best friends and at the same time we'll butt heads every now and then because we have the exact same personality," Ashlee explained. "She was also the younger sister of two sisters. She was the crazy one — not the party-crazy one, just the crazy one. And then she got married at 18."

But Tina also gets something out of hanging out with her younger rock star daughter — Ashlee has helped her mom stay in touch with her inner teenager! "My mom loves rock," Ashlee told the *New York Times*. "She jams to my CD, it's so cute. I think my mom had rock living in her, so now I kind of got to open her up to it."

The New Boy

In the third episode of *The Ashlee Simpson Show*, Ashlee flees Los Angeles and the problems with making her record to appear in her friend Ryan

Cabrera's music video. Ryan, a native of Dallas, Texas, was the first client that Joe Simpson signed up to his budding management company.

As Ryan started working with Joe and became a fixture around the Simpson household — even living there for a time — he and Ashlee became best friends. So it was no surprise that Ryan wanted her to be in his first music video.

In Ryan's video "On the Way Down," Ashlee appears as a bartender in a club who's obviously drawn to the young singer and his music. She also appears goofing around with Ryan on the streets of Austin, looking very much like a younger Cameron Diaz in a fun little wool hat with a pom-pom! The pair hold hands, cuddle, climb a tree, and give each other piggyback rides — so cute!

Viewers of *The Ashlee Simpson Show* got the behind-the-scenes scoop on the making of the video as Ashlee struggled against a very early call time and a traumatic bad hair day. However, by the time the cameras start rolling, Ashlee's mood changed. Something new and exciting was in the air. Were those real romantic sparks flying between Ashlee and the young guitarist?

When the two best friends shared an on-camera

kiss for the video, the director had a hard time getting them to stop! And no one was probably more surprised than Ryan when Ashlee pinned him against the wall for a real-life kiss.

Josh who? It looked like Ashlee had finally found a cure for her broken heart.

It's a Hit!

But more than any romantic drama, Ashlee's sunny personality was the glue that held together all the various people in her life and made new viewers of *The Ashlee Simpson Show* tune in to see what would happen next. "Ashlee's got a tremendous personality," Geffen Records president Jordan Schur told the Associated Press. "People gravitate toward that. They want to watch her and listen to her music."

In the first week, more than 2.9 million viewers tuned in to *The Ashlee Simpson Show*, according to *Entertainment Weekly*. In the following weeks, the numbers continued to grow, eventually making Ashlee's show more popular than the episodes of Jessica and Nick's reality series, *Newlyweds*, which preceded it each week. By the time Ashlee's show completed its run, more than 50 million viewers had tuned in at least once, making *The Ashlee Simpson Show* the number one highest-rated show on cable, according to a report on PR Newswire. "I've been surprised with the ratings and everything," Ashlee told the *New York Daily News*. "I didn't know it would do that well."

Ashlee found that even she was fascinated by the show. "Every episode surprises me. I'm like, 'Did I really do that?'" she confessed during an MSN Internet chat. "I didn't get to see them before they aired."

"It was definitely interesting having cameras on me all the time, but it was worth it," she added. "The MTV crew became my close friends so we had a lot of fun."

On a personal level, watching the show became like reading the pages of Ashlee's diary. "What's cool is this whole experience is being recorded, everything from her getting her record deal through making the album," Tina told the *Los Angeles Times*.

"Fifteen years from now, I'll be able to show my kids when I signed my record deal," Ashlee added. "And the boyfriends I went through."

"I think it's been pretty accurate," Ashlee told

the *Chicago Tribune*. "Those are my best friends you see me with, and that's how my life is, and that's how it is making a record. It even shows the bad days in the studio. That's why I was so happy with it, because I don't look perfect."

CHAPTER 6
Behind the Music

Making an album of music might sound like a lot of fun, but it's a lot harder than it appears — even if you've watched every episode of *Making the Band*. For Ashlee, who began recording *Autobiography* in early 2004, it was the moment when she could either succeed, or fail miserably. And that was a lot of pressure bearing down on her slim shoulders. To make matters worse, thanks to the MTV cameras from *The Ashlee Simpson Show*, the whole world was there to watch. "There's extra pressure because you're like, 'OK, I'm trying to lay my heart down and they're right there,'" Ashlee confessed to MTV. "It's kind of weird."

One thing was certain: Ashlee wanted to forge her own musical path, separate from the one Jessica had already carved out for herself. "I am so proud of

Jessica," Ashlee told *Billboard* columnist Chuck Taylor. "She is an amazing artist with a beautiful voice. But I have never listened to the kind of music that she does. We're both doing music — but in very different ways."

In creating her debut album, Ashlee wanted to draw upon the music, mostly made by women rockers, that she loved while growing up. Those influences — which varied from the Pretenders' lead singer, Chrissie Hynde, to hard-living sixties legend Janis Joplin and from Fleetwood Mac's witchy woman, Stevie Nicks, to Blondie's tough girl, Deborah Harry, and eighties icon Pat Benatar — were the basis of the sound she was trying to capture. "These women were sexy and rocked," explained Ashlee. "They just had this strong characteristic about them. Tough girls. I like that. They had something to say, and I like it when people really do speak truly."

To help Ashlee develop her sound, her record company found her a producer famous for his work with female rockers. John Shanks had produced hits for Michelle Branch, Sheryl Crow, and Alanis Morissette. He encouraged Ashlee to find her own unique voice.

"I just wanted to go in and make a record and not worry about what genre it would be," Ashlee told a teen magazine. "I went in to have a good time and I did. It's a rock record, with a cool edge to it."

Ashlee also appreciated how special it was for a young artist like herself to have so much influence on her debut album. So many performers — even older ones — don't get that same opportunity. But Ashlee clearly had something special that the record executives at Geffen recognized and appreciated. "My label was amazing because they really let me have my hands in there," Ashlee exclaimed. "I really got to write a lot. It was cool."

Of course, Ashlee didn't write her first album alone. To teach her more about songwriting and help her organize her ideas into catchy verses, chorus, and melody, John introduced Ashlee to some of today's top songwriters. "I did a song called 'Unreachable' with Stan [Frazier] from Sugar Ray and Steve Fox," Ashlee said during an Internet chat on MSN. "I've been a huge fan of Sugar Ray for a while, so that was cool. I also cowrote with the guys from Good Charlotte and John Feldmann from Goldfinger and that was fun. I did three songs with them. It's just fun to collaborate with people that are like artists, and kind of have a different perspective."

But the songwriters were careful not to dilute

Ashlee's passion for her songs. When the songs from *Autobiography* come on the radio, they're really a true reflection of the hopes, dreams, fears, and worries of Ashlee, not some older guy trying to imagine what life is like for a young woman. "I came up with, like, the whole entire concept of the song — lyrically and everything," Ashlee explained in an interview. "To me, writing is a very important thing. It's, like, what I've always done and what I've always loved to do. It was a big part of my wanting to do a record."

"Shadow"

One of the songs that earns the most attention on *Autobiography* is "Shadow," the tune where Ashlee explores her feelings about being the younger sister of a glamorous, talented beauty like Jessica Simpson. Because the song deals with a subject that most people experience at least once in their lives — sibling rivalry — it has quickly become a fan favorite. Plus, people have always been curious about discovering what Ashlee *really* thinks of her successful older sister.

Well, it turned out to be complicated, like most family situations are. Because Jessica had expressed her singing ability very early in life, her parents had groomed her for stardom from a very young age. Watching as her older sister — who was also always the sweet-tempered, "good girl" of the family — got all the attention hurt Ashlee's feelings when she was a kid. Although she'd long ago brushed away those feelings of envy and hurt, Ashlee found herself having to face her old doubts as she tried to write "Shadow."

"I was dealing with my inner demons and my inner voices in my head," Ashlee explained to the *New York Times*. "It wasn't necessarily my parents being bad parents. It was just things that I battled in my head. Feeling second best, or feeling that they didn't love me."

But "Shadow" explores more than just jealousy. Ashlee also used the song to apologize to her family for all the times when she felt angry that Jessica was getting all the attention. She used the song to send a special thank-you message to her family for letting her find her own way out from behind her sister's shadow.

"The song's saying: 'Guys, I apologize, if I ever put you through hell. I love you and love my life, and thank you for letting me be myself, even though I messed up at times,'" Ashlee explained to an interviewer.

"It's about my sister and it's about finding my identity and finding who I am as a person," she told MTV. "It's about what I'm gonna be and all that kind of stuff. There was a while where I felt I was so sorry for everything and I was just like, 'Oh my God, I'm so sorry!' And basically, it's like I'm stepping up and saying I have nothing to be sorry for, you know what I mean? It's about coming into my own."

How did Jessica feel about being the subject of one of Ashlee's most-talked-about songs? She was thrilled, excited, and tremendously proud of her little sister. "When my sister heard the song 'Shadow,' she cried and said, 'That's the most beautiful song I ever heard,'" Ashlee said during an MSN chat. Jessica still calls "Shadow" one of her favorite songs on *Autobiography*. "She was in her dressing room the other day and she was singing it," said Ashlee. "My family is very proud."

"Giving It All Away"

Another of the songs that Ashlee is particularly proud of is "Giving It All Away," a tune that she hopes will really speak to teenagers who are confused and angered by the problems that life can unexpectedly place on them.

"It's just sort of about life," Ashlee explained to an interviewer. "It talks about a broken family — it's not just talking about my family. It just talks about a bunch of friends in different situations and how they just give themselves away. I talk about myself and say like, 'I'm broken and I'm picking up the pieces.'"

Ashlee hopes that everyone will hear her message of hope in the lyrics. After all, tomorrow really is another day. "It says hold on to your life and don't give that away," she explains. "It's really saying don't just give yourself away because there's so much to look forward to. It's a song I was really proud of."

Nothing makes Ashlee happier than finding out that a fan has heard her message of hope and healing in one of her songs like "Giving It All Away." "It's just a huge compliment," Ashlee commented during an MSN chat. "It definitely does have to do with healing and looking for hope in a situation and coming out stronger. Everyone has things they deal with and at the end of the day, it's learning a lesson about yourself."

Ashlee dyed her hair from blond to brunette and doesn't plan on going back. "I think I looked really young with blond hair.... Now, I feel more womanly."

Ashlee had a blast at the 2004 Teen Choice Awards, winning both the Choice Fresh Face and Choice Song of the Summer for "Pieces of Me."

No longer in the shadows, blond Ashlee stands side by side with big sister, Jessica.

Ashlee says she and Jessica are "like night and day." While they have different taste in music and fashion, they love and support each other all the way.

Ashlee was thrilled to present a 2004 MTV Video Music Award with her crush Dave Navarro. She congratulated Carmen Electra on nabbing such a perfect husband. "He's so cute because he loves Carmen so much."

Ashlee has worked hard to become comfortable onstage. She credits her acting experiences with helping her to feel the emotions of her songs.

Ashlee poses with on-again, off-again but always best friend, Ryan Cabrera.

Ashlee admits to a casual style: "I tend to put a lot of random things together." She credits her mom, Tina, with helping make her style more "TV friendly."

Her shirt may say "New York Doll," but Ashlee's heart is definitely still in Texas.

Much of Ashlee's musical inspiration comes from women rockers like Janis Joplin and Chrissie Hynde, who she grew up listening to. "These women were sexy and rocked," Ashlee explains.

"La La"

Ashlee had a lot of fun recording the rocker "La La," a song that she expected would ignite a little bit of controversy. "I've always kind of liked to shock people," she told the *Los Angeles Times*. "With my record, I wasn't afraid to be myself."

In the song, Ashlee sings about pretending to be an alley cat and a French maid. "There's a lot of sarcasm in that song," she says. "I decided to make a joke about it. It's one of the songs you can dance around to."

To really let loose and bring out that wild and crazy part of herself, Ashlee dressed up to record "La La." "I must have looked like a crazy lady," Ashlee confessed during an interview. "I recorded it in my underwear and a tank top and a scarf. I dressed myself and it was so funny. We were having the best time."

"Unreachable"

Naturally, Ashlee's traumatic breakup with Josh became a big subject to write about on *Autobiography*. The song "Unreachable" addresses her feelings of hopelessness over dating someone so self-absorbed.

"It was actually good for me," she told *USA Today*. In fact, writing "Unreachable" made her see the whole relationship more clearly. "It's like, 'Oh, that's why I'm not with him,'" she said. "Because he's a jerk!'"

But Ashlee didn't actually set out to write a song to trash Josh, or any other person for that matter. "I don't want it to look like I'm a hard person and I hate my boyfriend," she told an interviewer. "I wanted it to be very honest. With everything on the record, it's just very honest and very me. I was very true to my emotions. I hurt and I wasn't afraid to say that I was hurting and how I got over it. It was as if I was standing up saying, 'Look, here I am, I just want someone to love me for me.'"

"Undiscovered"

Another song that addresses her breakup with Josh is "Undiscovered," the final track on the album. In this heartbreaking tune — which musically sounds a lot like the super group U2 — Ashlee sings "I need you" and begs her ex not to walk out the door. She explained that the emotional meltdown heard at the end of the song is completely real. "I think it's my favorite song on the record," she told a reporter.

"Whenever I did the song in the studio, it was just real emotional. It was just happening and real."

"We were all in the studio and I was just on the mic and it was happening," she continued. "I just bawled my eyes out on it. When I was finished, everyone said, 'God, that has to be on your album.'"

For Ashlee, recording "Undiscovered" was a way of saying good-bye to Josh. "It felt like the time to let go of my first love," she said. "Just let go and move on."

"Pieces of Me"

On a happier note, Ashley wrote her biggest hit, "Pieces of Me," for her new sometimes boyfriend and always best friend, Ryan Cabrera. "[The song] is about being so stressed out and then at the end of the day seeing him and it all goes away," she said.

After her relationship with Josh ended so disastrously, Ashlee was happy to be with a guy as caring and affectionate as Ryan. To show how much his kindness meant to her, she wrote him the song "Pieces of Me." "You know, before we started dating, we were best friends for a really long time," Ashlee explained. "I had gotten out of the Josh situation and . . . it was like, 'Oh my gosh. It just feels good to know that I can be with somebody who's just real and who's nice.'"

One of the reasons Ashlee and Ryan worked together as a couple is that because they were both singers, they could understand what the other one was dealing with. "He had just finished making his record," Ashlee explained. "There's always a lot of stress when you make a record, but he was just always there for me. You know, he's just a good person."

The best part was playing "Pieces of Me" for Ryan the very first time. It was a moment that Ashlee will never forget. "I finished the song and I was like, 'I wrote a song about you,'" she recalled. "I was so excited!"

How did Ryan react? "I think he said, 'Oh, baby, you're so cute,' and gave me a big hug," Ashlee said during an MSN chat on the Internet. "He was so excited."*

By the time that Ashlee had finished writing and recording *Autobiography*, she felt as if she had really accomplished something special. "Finishing my album was amazing," she said during an Internet chat with fans. "It felt like a journey. When I

*In fact, "Pieces of Me" ended up being Ryan's favorite song on the whole album.

finished I felt I had grown stronger. I felt stronger because there were ex-boyfriends I dealt with. I looked at love differently."

Now, only one big question remained. Would the world love Ashlee's debut album as much as she did?

CHAPTER 7
Ashlee's Big Night

The streets around the ultrahip meatpacking district of New York City were still crowded with fans, tourists, and nightclub-goers when Ashlee made a fashionably late arrival at 10 P.M. with her parents at the nightclub PM. It was just one day before the release of her debut CD, *Autobiography*, but already everyone gathered at Ashlee's East Coast record release celebration was buzzing with the news that the CD would bow at number one on the *Billboard* album chart tomorrow.

Although it had been a long day for Ashlee — she'd been up since early that morning to make promotional appearances on *Good Morning America*, MTV's *TRL*, and several New York radio stations — she was in great spirits. For her New York party, Ashlee wore a black, Grecian-style Marni gown that made her look more like Helen of Troy than a rock princess. Accessorized with a whole lotta *bling*, including a stunning diamond solitaire necklace and some diamond bangle bracelets — borrowed from Jacob the Jeweler — and a pair of her favorite Marc Jacobs four-inch stilettos, Ashlee was ready to celebrate.

"I'm so excited," she told a reporter as she smiled for a flashing camera. "This has been, like, the most amazing day. You know, when you've been waiting for so long for something to happen and then when it does and it sinks in it's like, 'Oh my God.' It's incredible. I had an amazing day, I had an in-store [appearance] and there were just SO many people there and I mean everything was just very, very exciting."

A grinning Joe Simpson couldn't contain his pride in his youngest daughter's accomplishment. "There's no greater thing in the world than watching your children have dreams and then to be there when they come true," he said. "I've watched Ashlee since she was 14 be called 'Jessica's dancer' and 'Jessica's sister' or even 'that other girl from 7*th* Heaven,' but tonight she is no longer in the shadows. Tonight, she's the shadow-maker. She's standing tall and doing all the things she's always dreamed about."

Once inside the chic nightclub, Ashlee lost no time in staking out a prime table for herself, her bandmates, friends, and family. Her band, which her fans named Submission through an Internet contest, was comprised of lead guitarist Ray Brady, guitarist Braxton Olita, bass guitarist Zach Kennedy, and drummer Chris Fox. The guys were excited and had even sort of dressed up for the event. Two wore black shirts, two wore white, and all of them had put on clean jeans or dark chinos and their least-beaten-up Converse sneakers for the occasion. Also joining the gang, seated on top of the banquettes of their booth, was 'N Sync's Chris Kirkpatrick, who was Ray's roommate.

Although songs from *Autobiography* played over the stereo system for most of the party, Ashlee and the gang got really excited when the Black Eyed Peas' "Hey Mama" came on. Suddenly the whole gang was up and dancing on the table and the banquette, just having a good time. When a new song came on, Beyonce's "Naughty Girl," Ashlee cracked up her friends by doing her own version of the moves the Destiny's Child singer does in the video. Everyone was having such a good time. At some point, Ray even jumped on Chris's back and demanded a piggyback ride.

But when you're the star of the party, there are always new people to meet. Fortunately, Ashlee is so friendly and open that she didn't seem to mind being called away from her friends to chat with reporters or record company big shots. "Ashlee's friends with everybody in the whole world," commented her dad with a grin.

"So, Ashlee, how will you feel if your album debuts at number one tomorrow?" a reporter asked the night's big star.

"Oh my God," Ashlee said, tossing her dark bangs away from her blue-green eyes. "If it does I will be freaking out."

Waking Up a Star

Without a doubt, Ashlee woke up on the morning of July 28, 2004, the day of her album's official release, and freaked out. The news was good, very good.

"Ashlee Simpson may not have to go through life much longer being known primarily as Jessica's little sister," read an article in the *Chicago Tribune*. "The 19-year-old quasi-punkette's debut album, *Autobiography*, entered the sales charts at number one on Wednesday after selling 398,000 copies during its first week in stores."

"Ashlee Simpson has beaten her older sister — singer and MTV *Newlyweds* star Jessica Simpson — to No. 1 on the Billboard 200," crowed another report, this time in the *Hollywood Reporter*. "The younger Simpson . . . has made a name for herself outside her sister's shadow with her Geffen Records debut, *Autobiography*."

"Ashlee Simpson has done what her more famous sibling, Jessica, has failed to do: top the music charts. Simpson's album, *Autobiography*, hit number one in the U.S.," read another chart beat in Canada's *Toronto Sun*.

Even though Ashlee was told to expect the impossible, she had a hard time believing it was true. "Before my album came out, I was so happy, so content," she told a reporter from the *New York Times*. "I hit a place where I just thought, 'Wow, I've come into my own. I'm growing up.' Then the album came out — and it's doing really well. It's shocking and amazing. I cried on the airplane the other day and I cried today."

Back on the Road

After her album was released, time on airplanes, crying or not, became a way of life for Ashlee. Her dad and Geffen Records decided that Ashlee would never perform to backing tapes, so she traveled with her band, Submission, a bunch of young, cool guys who learned the songs from her album and became her new best friends on the road.

Braxton Olita, an 18-year-old from Hawaii, auditioned for Submission in March 2004 and by May was already on Ashlee's promotional tour. The 2003 high school graduate joined guitarist Ray Brady, Zach Kennedy on bass guitar, and drummer Chris Fox as Ashlee's traveling band.

"It's been just unreal in every way," Braxton told his hometown newspaper. "It's a dream of just anyone who can appreciate music."

For Ashlee, her band provided friends who she could relate to and hang around with. She grew particularly close to Ray, who was Ashlee's musical director as well as one of the first people hired for Submission. "Since I always have my band with me, I'm surrounded by really fun people," Ashlee said during an MSN live chat. "At Six Flags, we rode the Superman ride like six times and had so much fun.

I try to surround myself with positive, happy people to keep me grounded."

But playtime never lasted for very long. Ashlee and Submission played their first live show together for an audience of record company big-wigs, journalists, family, and friends in Los Angeles. Ashlee's old friend *Malcolm in the Middle*'s Frankie Muniz, on whose show Ashlee received her first acting break, was there to lend moral support.

"The first time I was onstage as a music artist, I was very nervous," Ashlee admitted during an MSN chat. "I had my good friends with me and butterflies before I went on. But after a while, I loved it. It was like nerves and then I got onstage and I was like, 'Am I really here?' Like an out-of-body experience."

Ashlee and Submission's second gig together was also a really big, important, and potentially scary one. Ashlee and the boys played "Pieces of Me" on *The Tonight Show with Jay Leno* for an audience of millions. "I feel like I've been thrown into the fire," Ashlee admitted to the *Chicago Tribune*. "My second show ever was performing on *Jay Leno*!"

Of course, Ashlee did a wonderful job on *The Tonight Show*, but few knew how much she had to overcome to get there. Joe Simpson explained to *In Touch* that Ashlee had to work a lot harder than her sister to become comfortable onstage. "Ashlee has actually always been the entertainer in the family, as far as acting and doing plays," explained Joe. "She was crazy [in real life] but when Ashlee got onstage, she became this shy little girl. We had to work really hard."

To help her bring out her very best as a performer, Ashlee learned to draw on her acting experience to really feel the emotions of the songs. "My acting experience really helped me get into the characters of the songs and be in the moment," Ashlee explained to MTV. "I was able to go back to the events I'm singing about and bring them to life."

For Ashlee and the band, there were some amazing, memorable moments, like their first appearance on *The Late Show with David Letterman*. "All of us in the band are really starting to feel comfortable onstage together and it shows in the performance," Zach, Submission's bassist, wrote on Ashlee's website. "The highlight of the day goes to Ray jamming with [*Late Show* musical director] Paul Shaffer during our sound check. Ashlee looked amazing and we had a blast."

Other stops on the tour didn't go quite as well.

"We played a show on a pier in the middle of a lake," Ashlee wrote on her website in July 2004. "It poured down raining but we went on three hours late!"

But no matter where Ashlee and her band traveled, she was able to rely on her fans being there to support her and love her all the way.

Meeting the Fans

One of Ashlee's most memorable performances was doing a preshow mini-concert at the MTV 2004 Video Music Awards in Miami. "Because you're there with a bunch of fans, it's like a real show," she enthused to *USA Today*. Although it was cool to perform in front of television cameras for millions of viewers, Ashlee explained that it was the live fans in the audience who really made each show special.

"I think the most rewarding is playing shows now while fans are singing my songs at the top of their lungs with me," Ashlee said during an MSN chat. "It's the coolest feeling, and I always get chills. That's when everything is worth it. It's very cool."

Although Ashlee had already seen her sister's popularity soar and even earned some fan letters and fansites of her own through her role on 7th *Heaven*, the number of people who suddenly knew her name was shocking and thrilling. Ashlee was eternally grateful for them for making her feel at home no matter where in the United States she wandered. "These fans come up at my in-store, and they talk about how nice it is to see a girl talk about heartbreak, and how it's gotten them through theirs," Ashlee explained during an interview. "Touching those people is amazing to me."

Easygoing Ashlee hasn't met a fan she didn't enjoy visiting with. "I think my fans are so cool and so supportive," she added during an MSN chat. "I appreciate it so much. Every time I get to meet them it's so fun! Everyone I met is so cool."

It didn't even trouble Ashlee when people who watched *The Ashlee Simpson Show* acted like they knew everything about her real life. She even received some advice from fans on her love life! "It's crazy . . . everyone is like, 'I know what's going on in your life' and 'oh my god, your ex-boyfriend is a dork!' It's so funny," Ashlee told a reporter. "I think it's cool because [fans] actually get to meet the people that the songs are written about and I really thought that was a cool thing."

In July 2004, an overwhelmed Ashlee wrote a

special thank-you note to her fans on her website! "This past week has been so exciting for me," Ashlee wrote. "I never could have imagined the success that the album has had in my wildest dreams, and it's all because of you guys. THANK YOU SO MUCH!!! My in-stores have been so cool for me because I finally get to meet ya'll face-to-face. . . . I LOVE MY FANS! I appreciate the time that you all have taken to come see me, and it means the world to me. I wish I could stay and meet every single one of you!! You guys have been so supportive, and I cannot begin to thank ya'll enough. I have the best fans in the world!"

Love Rumors!

Naturally, as soon as Ashlee became the new "it" girl, everyone wanted to know who she was dating. While her best friend, Ryan Cabrera, still remains in the picture, he and Ashlee's complicated schedules and commitments to their careers often keep them apart. The couple displayed a knack for confusing everyone by breaking up and getting back together a bunch of times. "I'm actually not dating anybody," Ashlee told *USA Today* in July 2004. "Ryan Cabrera and I were dating, but we broke up. Right now I'm single and I'm truly enjoying it."

A little while later, Ashlee and Ryan were back together again. "We broke up for like two weeks, but it didn't last," Ashlee happily told a reporter. "We like each other too much. We've been together for five months."

Another month later, the pair was separated again. "I'm too busy and young to date seriously," Ashlee told a foreign reporter while on tour in Singapore. "I'm young and I just want to have fun. Besides, I'm working too much right now for a serious relationship."

As Ashlee and Ryan continue to keep everyone guessing, one thing is for certain: These two haven't written the final chapter in their love story yet! It's definitely "to be continued!"

But while Ryan was busy traveling the country as Jessica's opening act, Ashlee was left to her own devices. And naturally, when someone is suddenly as huge a star as Ashlee, it's likely that people will gossip.

One of the earliest rumors was about Ashlee and Ray Brady, her music director and lead guitarist. Since she spends so much time with her band, Submission, it's no surprise that gossip circulated about Ashlee and Ray getting very close. But the bandmates laughed it off.

Then, for a while before he began his high-profile romance with heiress Paris Hilton, Backstreet Boys' singer Nick Carter was rumored to be involved with Ashlee. That gossip really made the singer laugh. "No! That is SO random," she told *USA Today*. "When I heard that, I was dying laughing."

Ashlee also dismissed suggestions that she had been romantically involved with MTV personality Carson Daly, who at 31 is 11 years older than her. Ick!

However, Ashlee did get cozy with a different, more age-appropriate MTV personality. She and *TRL*'s host Damien Fahey, 24, spent a cuddly night dancing this close at the hip New York spot Crobar in June 2004. The explanation? Ashlee and Damien are old friends. They worked together in the summer of 2003 when Ashlee helped cohost the MTV beach house in the Hamptons!

Like most girls her age, Ashlee has also confessed to a couple of celebrity crushes — the only difference is that she gets to meet most of them. "I just think the lead singer of Maroon 5 is sooo hot," Ashlee squealed to *In Touch*, sounding like any normal young woman. She couldn't help expressing her admiration for the L.A.-based band's singer, Adam Levine. "When he performs, it is so sexy that it is like the most amazing thing."

Ashlee also expressed her crush on former Red Hot Chili Peppers guitarist Dave Navarro, and credits fellow MTV reality star Carmen Electra for choosing a perfect husband in him. Ashlee met them both when she presented an award with Dave at the 2004 MTV Movie Awards. "I thought Dave Navarro was really hot," she told a reporter. "He's so cute because he loves Carmen so much. I was just like, 'This is the cutest thing ever.' It made me want that someday. I told him, 'I want to meet somebody like you who loves me as much as you love your wife.'"

Frequent Fliers

Just because *Autobiography* hit number one in the United States didn't mean that all of Ashlee's hard work was done. It was totally the opposite! After conquering the American record charts, Ashlee and Submission packed their bags to start spreading their music overseas too.

At the end of the summer — after Ashlee won Choice Fresh Face and Choice Song of Summer for

"Pieces of Me" at the 2004 Teen Choice Awards —
Submission and their lead singer headed for
Singapore and Japan.

First they were scheduled to appear at the
Singapore Fireworks Festival and at another show
at a skate park sponsored by MTV. "We are having
a blast!" wrote Zach on Ashlee's official website. "We
played two shows in Singapore and they were so
much fun. Chris found out that in Singapore he is
considered 'hotter than Josh Hartnett.'"

But it was also hard work. During most of her
four-day stay, Ashlee barely had time to wander far
from her room at the Ritz-Carlton Hotel. "Besides
the shows I played, I mostly did interviews," she
told a local newspaper. "I didn't get to shop or anything."

Next Ashlee and the group were off to
Tokyo, Japan, where they enjoyed two days of free
time — and lots of shopping to make up for
Singapore — before playing two dates. But it was a
long time to be so very far from home and the crew
confessed to a touch of homesickness. "Even though
we are having an experience of a lifetime, we miss
our friends and family so much, and of course,
American food," wrote Zach on the website.

In early September, Ashlee and the boys of

Submission came back for a quick break at home in California (all the boys in the band and, of course, Ashlee, currently call Southern California home). Then it was time to pack the bags again for the flight to Europe. Ashlee and Submission played shows in Cologne, Germany — where they overnighted in a castle that was supposed to be haunted — Berlin, and finally London, England.

In all, their first trip to Europe provided a lot of memories and tons of life experiences that none of them would ever forget. "Germany and England couldn't have been any better," wrote Zach on Ashlee's official website. "We had so much fun!"

CHAPTER 8
The Future

As 2004, the most exciting and memorable year Ashlee had ever experienced, drew rapidly to a close, the singer was faced with a lot of choices. The success of her album, *Autobiography*, brought Ashlee to the attention of a lot of people who offered her everything from movie roles to opportunities to become a spokesperson for new products. But for Ashlee, the music came first.

Touring with Ryan

The green-eyed singer was also excited to do a bunch of free concerts for high school students. Winners of the nationwide Rock, Vote, and Win contest each received a free concert at their school by Ashlee Simpson and Ryan Cabrera. Over the fall, the singers performed shows in Fountain Valley and Los Angeles, California; Lancaster, Pennsylvania; Cleveland and Cincinnati, Ohio; Salt Lake City, Utah; Tucson, Arizona; and Demarest, New Jersey.

For Ashlee, performing and meeting fans at all the schools was incredible. It was also great to be seeing a lot more of Ryan again. "He has been my best friend for a long time," she told an interviewer.

Ryan, meanwhile, tried to explain their complicated relationship to an interviewer from *USA Today*. "When we get to see each other, it's awesome," he said. "We're together, but we're concentrating on being friends right now. We're best friends and have a great relationship."

Still, the wild-haired singer doesn't consider himself a single guy. "I'm not out looking for another girl, and she's not out looking for another guy," he explained. "It's not like we're 'together' or 'not together.'"

Ashlee's Most Embarrassing Moment

One of the reasons that live musical performances are so electrifying is that anything can happen. Ashlee found that out the hard way when she was scheduled to perform on *Saturday Night Live* in late October 2004.

For the young singer, the trouble began in rehearsals the afternoon before what would be her most embarrassing performance ever. "The day of *Saturday Night Live*, I completely lost my voice," Ashlee confessed to interviewer Carson Daly. "Four hours before the show, *I lost my voice.*"

A witness to Ashlee's dress rehearsal for the show explained that Ashlee's vocal problems were evident to everyone backstage. "Her voice was horrible, and everybody was commenting on it during the dress rehearsal," said a backstage witness.

A doctor, the same one who usually attends to veteran stage performer Wayne Newton, was called in to figure out what was wrong. It was determined that Ashlee's acid reflux disease — a severe case of heartburn the singer has suffered from for some time — was causing swelling of her vocal chords and laryngitis. The doctor warned Ashlee against singing — adding that if she tried, she could permanently damage her vocal chords.

But Ashlee was reluctant to cancel her appearance on *Saturday Night Live*, a series famous for showcasing the hottest musical acts over the past 30 years. "I can't cancel something like *SNL*,"

Ashlee reportedly wrote to her fans on her website after the controversy. "You and I know that even if I synched on it or not, I'd still get seen by millions, maybe even make a few more fans."

Joe Simpson says that it was his decision to let Ashlee and the band go on with the show, using a backing tape to substitute for Ashlee's problematic voice. Although many people frown on lip-synching, Joe explained after the controversy that almost every performer is forced to do it now and then. "Every artist that I know in this business has had vocal problems at some time — from Celine [Dion] on down," Joe told Ryan Seacrest in a radio interview. "So you've got to do what you've got to do."

"I had never done it once," Ashlee told Katie Couric on *Today*. "My dad was like, 'Honey, you have to do it.' He put my vocal doctor on the phone with me. 'You have to. (Singing) will ruin your vocal chords.'"

Although she was singing along to a tape, Ashlee's performance of "Pieces of Me" went off without a problem. It was during her second song of the night that things got out of control. She was supposed to be performing her new single, "Autobiography," but when Ashlee took the stage, the music started for her song "Pieces of Me." Worse yet,

83

Ashlee's voice could be heard singing "Pieces of Me," but she wasn't even holding the microphone near her mouth!

Clearly embarrassed and confused, Ashlee performed sort of a jig, dancing around the stage as the band gamely played along with the music. After a few moments of floundering around onstage, Ashlee fled the scene. The band continued to play "Pieces of Me" for a few moments more, and then the show cut to a commercial.

At the end of the show, Ashlee bravely returned to the stage with *SNL*'s guest host, Jude Law. "What can I say?" Jude said, trying to soften what had just happened. "Live TV."

"Exactly," added Ashlee. "I feel so bad. My band started playing the wrong song. I didn't know what to do so I thought I'd do a hoedown."

Two days later, Ashlee tried to explain to her fans on her website. "I'll hold my head high and say I think it was silly of me to do it, silly of me to blame the band. I was just so . . . embarrassed," she added. "But I don't think it did me much harm, and people will see that soon."

In the end, it didn't harm Ashlee's band either. Although it was determined that Ashlee's drummer pushed the wrong button on *SNL*, which played the wrong song, he wasn't fired. "I love my drummer to death," Ashlee told Katie. "It was the wrong button he pushed. I was sick and things happen."

Two nights later, Ashlee and the band redeemed themselves when they performed live at NBC's Radio Music Awards — but first, the singer had a cortisone shot to make sure that her acid reflux condition wouldn't become an issue again.

Ashlee also used the opportunity to poke a little fun at the controversy. "It's the wrong song!" she yelled to the band as they began to play. She then turned to the crowd and the millions of people watching her on live TV. "Only kidding," Ashlee said before launching into a terrific live performance of "Autobiography."

"I figured, why not make a joke about it," she told Katie Couric. "I am not worried about it. I know that things happen and not everybody is perfect. You can't help it if you lose your voice. It doesn't mean you can't sing or don't write your own music."

Ashlee's true-blue fans agreed with her. "I think what happened only makes her more real," a fan from New Jersey told a celebrity magazine. "As long as she keeps singing, lip-synching or not, she'll still be liked."

Making Movies

Although Ashlee's music career couldn't be better, she was excited to suddenly receive all sorts of offers to do movies. "I can't wait to do a movie," she said during an MSN chat. "I've been looking forward to doing that for a while."

Though Ashlee made her big-screen debut in *The Hot Chick*, the 2002 hit comedy starring comedian Rob Schneider, that role only amounted to a handful of lines and about two minutes of screen time. While it was nothing to be ashamed of, Ashlee wanted something bigger and better for her next film project.

She found what she was looking for in a script called *Wannabe*, the story of a washed-up musician who moves to Los Angeles to try his hand at an acting career. "It's basically about musicians trying to find their way," Ashlee told MTV.

"There's a guy who gets too old to be a musician, and all of us become his fan club," she explained. "I play an actor."

Ashlee said she was drawn to the movie, which was scheduled to begin filming in November 2004, because it wasn't just another teen flick. "The movie involves music and actors," she explained. "It's going to be a great movie. [The studio] Lion's Gate does edgier films, so it's going to be really exciting."

Working with Jessica

In an effort to create her own identity, Ashlee has rarely worked with Jessica beyond a breath mint commercial and some small guest appearances on each other's MTV reality shows. And they never, ever sang together, although both sisters were constantly asked if a duet would ever happen.

Ashlee was the first to hint that it could. "I'd like to do something different for the both of us," Ashlee told the Associated Press. "Something where we can both step out of our styles."

Eventually, the sisters decided to collaborate on a new version of the holiday song "Little Drummer Boy," for Jessica's Christmas CD, *A Special Limited Edition Christmas Collection*, which was sold exclusively in 7-Eleven stores. "It's the record that Jessica has always dreamed of," Joe Simpson told *In Touch*. "It is the one genre that both of them can step outside and do something together because it's a Christmas song. Christmas is about family, tradition, and home — it's not about rock or pop."

87

Obviously, the sisters must have had a wonderful time recording "Little Drummer Boy" together, because Ashlee also agreed to appear on her sister's holiday TV special. Jessica and her husband, Nick Lachey, took television by storm in the spring of 2004 with *The Nick and Jessica Variety Hour*, a special that more than 11 million people tuned in to watch. The bubble-headed blond and her hunky hubby continued their streak with their ABC holiday special that was scheduled to air on December 2. "Christmas is a family time," said Ashlee.

But don't expect the musical Simpson sisters to ever do a tour together. "We don't have the same interests when it comes to music," Ashlee explained. "I actually don't think I would go on tour with her. I could have, but I chose not to because I love going out and watching her tour. It's great. It's the best I've ever, ever seen her in concert and she's awesome but I just didn't want to put ourselves in that situation." Still, there are times when Ashlee regrets her decision. "We wish we were on tour together at times," Ashlee admitted.

But the brunette Simpson sister hasn't ruled out working with Jessica on something completely different. "I would love to do a movie with Jessica or something," she said.

Small-screen Wonders

And speaking of other projects, just because Ashlee became a rock star didn't mean that she forgot her roots in television or the friends that she made during her time on *7th Heaven*. Although she was sad the day that the *7th Heaven* actors went back to work without her, she didn't rule out the possibility of bringing back Cecelia for a guest appearance on the hit WB show.

"Being on *7th Heaven* was so cool and such an awesome experience," she explained during an MSN live chat. "I love the cast. I'm going to miss them so much. I may do a guest appearance."

"I'm going to do a few episodes to end the character," she added to the *New York Post*.

Beyond *7th Heaven*, fans of *The Ashlee Simpson Show* were salivating for another season. After all, in the last episode, fans watched Ashlee on the cusp of stardom — *Autobiography* had just gone platinum and Ashlee was just starting to do talk shows and radio shows. Everyone wanted to see what happened next. Plus, everyone wanted more of Ashlee and Ryan's romance!

So, would Ashlee agree to do it? She had a difficult time deciding. "I think a second series would drive me crazy," she confessed to *Blender* magazine. But a few weeks later, she told MTV.com: "I'm pretty sure we'll do it."

Meanwhile, on Ashlee's website, her bandmate Zach sounded like he was very excited about the idea of being on the MTV reality show. "*Autobiography* is soaring up the charts and it looks like there might be a second season of the show!" he wrote.

If a second season does happen — and folks at MTV think it's very likely — there's one guy who won't be really thrilled to be back on camera: Ryan Cabrera! The choppy-haired guitarist learned the hard way that it's tough to have an intimate moment with your girlfriend while the camera is rolling. "The cameras got so close when we were making out — a foot from our faces — it freaked me out," he confessed in an interview.

More Music Too

While Ashlee has been on the road performing the songs from her multi-platinum, chart-topping debut CD, she's also been planning for the future. She isn't content to sit back on her success. "I am one of those people who takes a step forward, and then is like, 'What can I do next?'" she told MTV. "I am already thinking about the next record."

Ashlee is sure that recording her next album will be even more fun. She hadn't come together with her band, Submission, when *Autobiography* was recorded so she used a lot of different studio musicians. Now that she has new musician friends, she can't wait to bring Ray, Zach, Braxton, and Chris into the recording studio with her.

To prepare for the day she would start recording her sophomore album, Ashlee has been writing songs. "I am definitely still writing," Ashlee said during an MSN chat. "Every time I get a second to be alone, I always write." Ashlee never knows when she will be inspired to write. She has scrawled down ideas on long airplane rides, wrote lyrics on a napkin in a restaurant, even jotted down ideas on her hands or arms whenever she couldn't find paper. She's always on the lookout for that cool phrase or expression that will be the seed that grows into a new hit song. "Writing is something that is really important to me," she told MTV. "Everything that I'm going through, I'm writing about."

And don't be surprised if a certain special green-eyed boy — who Ashlee definitely must be writing songs about — shows up in the recording studio with Ashlee too. "We want to establish our own careers first," said Ashlee's on-again, off-again boyfriend and full-time best friend, Ryan Cabrera, "[but] we've talked about doing a duet together."

A Passion for Fashion

Over the year that Ashlee first became a star, fans couldn't help but comment on the really adorable clothes she wore. Although the five-foot-six rocker is most comfortable in jeans and a cute top, she's also a huge fan of Marc Jacobs, the designer.

Though her sister launched her own beauty and fragrance line, Dessert, in 2004, Ashlee thinks she'd be more inspired to do some fashion designing like one of her other favorite rock chicks, Gwen Stefani, who has a successful handbag and clothing line.

"I love clothes and I've always wanted to do my own thing," said Ashlee, who also enjoys prowling the vintage clothing racks for special one-of-a-kind discoveries. "I want to have my own clothing line. I would love to be a young, funky, more laid-back kind of Marc Jacobs."

New Newlyweds?

It's no secret that Ashlee's heart was broken into shreds when her boyfriend of two years, singer Josh Henderson, ended their relationship. Ashlee had admitted that she really expected to marry him one day.

Although she's formed a strong bond with Ryan, she's definitely not ready to settle down. She doubts that she will marry as young as her sister but she said that she would like to get married someday.

"I don't know when I'll marry. But eventually I do want that — to get married and have a house in Austin, a ranch, a recording studio at my ranch," she told the *New York Times*. "That whole world would be great. But you never know where life will take you."

Ashlee's not ready to look that far into the future. In fact, she can't even bring herself to adopt a dog because she's way too busy. "I would love to have a dog, but I don't think I can take care of one yet," she told a reporter. "My life is just now starting to get crazy and I'm traveling a lot. I'll have to wait until I'm more settled down."

Home in Los Angeles

When Ashlee does return from her world travels, the place she calls home is an apartment near Hollywood in Los Angeles that she shares with her best friend from Texas, aspiring actress Lauren Zelman. The two share a funky two-bedroom apartment, just 10 doors down the hallway from Ryan's apartment. "Moving here was like going to college," Ashlee told a celebrity magazine. "Ryan is my best friend, so I thought, 'Cool, I'll live there too.' Then a bunch of friends moved in and it became like *Melrose Place*.

"We have girl parties on Friday nights," she added. During Ashlee's girls' nights in, you're likely to find her with her friends watching romantic movies, eating popcorn, and drinking their favorite energy drink, Red Bull. Ashlee actually has Red Bull vending machines in her kitchen and her recording studio upstairs.

If Ryan is in town, he'll often come over for dinner. "I'm good at making tacos," said Ashlee. "Ryan and I have taco-offs to see whose are better." In case you're wondering, Ashlee said that Ryan often wins their *Iron Chef*-like culinary matches.

Ashlee's favorite room in her apartment isn't

the kitchen, however; it's her bedroom. The room is a jumble of colors and styles that perfectly match Ashlee's spunky personality. "My sister is good at decorating, but we have different styles," Ashlee explained. "I'm more random." But of everything in her room, Ashlee's favorite item is her wrought-iron bed that she found at a shop in Sherman Oaks, California. "When I see my room, I think, 'Aaahhh, I want to get in bed and sleep right now,'" she said. "It feels like home."

CHAPTER 9
Meet Jessica

Like her sister, Ashlee, Jessica was born to Tina and Joe Simpson, arriving in the world on July 10, 1980, in Abilene, Texas. From a very young age, the Simpsons' firstborn showed a passion for music, demonstrating a beautiful five-octave vocal range very early in life.

"Jessie has always been the singer," her dad proudly told a reporter. "Jessica was extremely shy with people, but when she got on a stage, she was crazy." Little Jessica gave her first public performance singing "Amazing Grace" in her father's church at five years old.

From a very early age, Jessica started reaching for stardom. As a youngster, she sang in the church choir and took classes in jazz, ballet, tap, and hip-hop dancing. At 14, she began taking vocal lessons with Linda Septien, a local coach, and even had a chance to sing the national anthem at a Dallas Stars game.

In addition to singing with her church youth group all through high school, Jessica also went into the recording studio for the first time in 1994 to record an album of Christian music. "I'd go to concerts and think, 'That's exactly what I want to do,'" this fan of divas like Whitney Houston and Mariah Carey told *People*.

But in many ways, Jessica was also a typical girl. She was a huge fan of New Kids on the Block and had such a big crush on NKOTB singer Jordan Knight that she named the family dog after him. She played Tiny Tim in her church's Christmas production of *Scrooge*, was a cheerleader in eighth grade for Richardson North Junior High's football team, the Vikings, and attended homecoming pep rallies with her friends at J.J. Pearce High School. She also was the lead in her high school's production of *A Chorus Line*.

Of course, Jessica was always a beauty, but she was also so sweet and nice that everyone liked her. She was crowned a Homecoming Princess in both 1995 and 1996.

She Almost Quit!

But Jessica's life wasn't just one easy jog up the ladder of popularity and success; she suffered some major disappointments too. She almost quit singing professionally after she failed to win a spot on *The New Mickey Mouse Club* at age 12, losing out to future stars Christina Aguilera and Britney Spears. "Everyone had head shots and had been on *Star Search*," said her father. "All Jessica had was a Polaroid." After watching Christina give an amazing, vocally perfect performance, Jessica lost her nerve. "I froze and forgot everything!" she recalls.

For Jessica, failing to become part of the cast was a devastating experience. "I wanted to give up, but my family kept me going," she said.

Jessica thought she might have finally received her big break a couple of years later when in 1994 she recorded an album of Christian music. Unfortunately for Jessica, the company she recorded for closed its doors before the album was ever released. Joe Simpson borrowed $10,000 from his mother to purchase the album masters and released the CD himself. He sold a lot of those albums himself too, peddling them whenever he traveled to other churches in Texas.

Stroke of Luck

But just a few months after Jessica finished high school, her luck changed. One of her homemade records had reached the desk of Sony Music executive Tommy Mottola, the man who had discovered Mariah Carey and made her a star. Jessica was invited to come to New York to try out for Mr. Mottola. "It was the most nerve-racking moment of my life," Jessica told a celebrity magazine. "I was supposed to sing two songs. After the first one, he said, 'Okay, you can have a seat.' I thought, 'Oh no, I blew it.'" Instead, the impressed star-maker signed Jessica to a recording contract on the spot.

Jessica's debut album, *Sweet Kisses*, was released in late 1999 and spawned a Top 10 single, "I Wanna Love You Forever." Suddenly, Jessica was thrust back into competition with her old *Mickey Mouse Club* rivals, Christiana Aguilera and Britney Spears, who also released their debut albums around the same time. But easygoing Jessica said she didn't think much about competing with the other girls. "I think there's room for everybody," she told a celebrity magazine.

"Hopefully I've differentiated myself from the whole up-tempo dance thing," she said. "I want people to fall in love with my voice before my image. I want to be a diva — like people-totally-respect-my-music diva, not diva like carry-my-diet-Coke-around."

Falling in Love

There are a lot of stories about how Jessica met her future husband, Nick Lachey, but the couple told a teen magazine the real story. "We met at a holiday parade. She was there with her family," Nick told *Tiger Beat*. "I'd heard she was a great singer and beautiful, but I was dating someone at the time."

He saw Jessica again a month later when she performed at a party for *Teen People*. "I watched her sing and saw the way people responded," he said, adding that he fell in love at that moment. "I'd broken up with the girl I was dating and I told my mom, 'Your mission for tonight is to get me hooked up with Jessica.' She did it too."

Within weeks of their first date, Nick was telling his bandmates in 98° that he would marry Jessica someday. But "someday" didn't happen quite so fast. The couple broke up once — their touring schedules were keeping them apart so much that it felt like they had to break up — but they couldn't forget each other. By the end of 2001, Jessica and Nick were back together and talking about plans for a wedding.

On October 26, 2002, Jessica walked down the aisle with Nick in a lavish Texas-sized wedding. And in a foreshadowing of her future *Newlyweds* reality TV series, she even let cameras for an *In Style* celebrity wedding television special record her wedding day. "I wanted my fans to see how happy we were and how real our love is," Jessica told *Newsweek*. "It was just a day I wanted to share."

Added Nick, who clearly couldn't predict his future reality-TV stardom: "Well, if the public is going to see anything, I'd much rather they see my wedding than some other things." Just you wait, Nick!

But even if the cameras weren't there, Jessica wouldn't have forgotten one detail of her wedding day. "The church was my favorite part of the entire day," she told *Newsweek*. "I walked in and I felt like I was Juliet in *Romeo and Juliet*. The colors and the flowers were amazing, and everyone you love, everyone you would die for, was sitting there watching you walk down the aisle. And standing there in front of you is the man that you are going to be with for the rest of your life."

Meet the Newlyweds

In 2003, Jessica and Nick let the world into their private life when *Newlyweds* began its run on MTV. The world watched as the young couple, total opposites who love each other anyway, tried to figure out how to live together — for better or for worse.

Along the way, the world fell in love with them too. Nick, the sensible one, came across as the most patient husband ever. "Nick takes care of me," Jessica told a teen magazine. "I'm a baby about a lot of things. He's real responsible and my head is all over the place."

But it was ditzy Jessica, who in one of her most famous moments wondered aloud if the tuna she was eating was chicken or fish, who became a superstar. Suddenly, everyone was laughing about her adorable ditziness, like the time she refused a buffalo chicken wing because she "doesn't eat buffalo." Or when she took her Louis Vuitton handbag on a camping trip in the woods.

"I think *Newlyweds* is hysterical," Ashlee told MTV. "I think the most amazing thing that Jessica has done for her career was *Newlyweds* because people needed to see that. She's gorgeous, but she's just normal like anybody else, you know?"

The only thing that sometimes made Ashlee angry was when people said her sister was stupid. "Everybody makes stupid comments, and if they had cameras with them day in and day out, you would see all the stupid things that come out of their mouths, too," Ashlee told the *Hollywood Reporter*. "We know that she is a bright girl and incredibly intelligent in real life."

"I think that she is charming and adorable and very bright," Ashlee added to another reporter. "Jessica has always said comments like that, so I didn't think anything of it. We all think stupid things from time to time . . . the fact that she says them makes her more endearing."

Fortunately, Nick and Jessica were able to laugh at the jokes about Jessica's smarts that were thrown their way after *Newlyweds* became a sensation. "Sometimes it's hard not to take offense when you're doing an interview and someone's being pretty hard on your wife," Nick told TV host Ryan Seacrest. "But the one thing I'll give Jessica, she's had a great attitude about it from day one. We knew going in that we were opening ourselves up to public opinion and criticism. And we've been very good, I think, about having a sense of humor."

"I think that's totally important, just to laugh with everybody else," added Jessica.

Sibling Rivalry

Up until Ashlee's album was released in 2004, Jessica was the star of the family while her younger sister was relegated to a background role as her sister's backup dancer, friend, and constant cheerleader. That all changed when the world had a chance to see what Ashlee was all about and how different she was from her blond sister. "I knew people were going to say, 'Oh my gosh, you're trying to be like your sister.' But I'm like, 'No.'" Ashlee told MTV.

"I am who I am and Jessica is who she is," Ashlee told another interviewer. "We're very different people — different people who both love each other so much. But we're so not the same."

Jessica loves designer clothing and really glamorous fashion, while Ashlee's look is more grungy and down-to-earth. Jessica is shy around strangers; Ashlee can talk to anyone, anywhere at any time. "Jessica and I are like night and day," Ashlee told *Entertainment Weekly*. "She grew up listening to Celine Dion and Mariah Carey. I grew up listening to Alanis Morissette and Green Day."

But on the really important things, Ashlee and Jessica are totally in tune. "We don't have the same interests when it comes to music or anything like that," explained Ashlee. "But Jessica loves my music; she listens to my CD before she goes onstage. And I go to concerts of hers because I love to watch her. We are real supportive, very, very supportive."

Jessica showed her support by praising Ashlee's success in paving her own way to fame as a singer. "I always say that Ashlee's not following in my footsteps, she's making footsteps of her own — because she's not becoming me by any means," Jessica told *20/20*.

Jessica also gives her little sister high marks for her ability to charm the whole world. "Ashlee can have such a great personality and have everybody be in love with her, every guy lined around the corner," said Jessica.

But as the younger sister, Ashlee owes Jessica. She did learn some valuable lessons watching what Jessica went through to become a successful singer. "Jessica is always, no matter what she's been through, she's always stayed true to herself, and that's what I look up to," said Ashlee in an interview.

"The one thing Jessica has really done for me is that she shows me that you don't have to be something else," Ashlee told another reporter. "You just be yourself. People really do want to see you be real."

But Jessica refuses to take credit for any lessons she may have taught her little sister. "Ashlee doesn't need any advice," Jessica told a reporter from the Associated Press. "Ashlee is very much an observer. She sees decisions that I've made that are good, and decisions I've made that are bad. She's definitely well set up."

But there is one person that Ashlee turns to for advice — her brother-in-law, Jessica's husband, Nick. "Every time I have boyfriend trouble, he gives me the right answer: 'Make the guy jealous,'" Ashlee confided to *People*.

And while Jessica, for her part, doesn't ever try to tell Ashlee what do to, she has tried her best to protect her little sister and steer her in the right direction. Ashlee told a story of how Jessica subtly talked her out of getting a star-shaped tattoo on her foot. Instead of simply telling Ashlee not to do it, Jessica went out and bought her sister a gift from Tiffany & Co. "Here you go, a key chain with a star on it," Jessica told Ashlee when she gave her the unexpected present. "I'm giving you this so you don't get that tattoo."

Despite how close and supportive the Simpson

sisters are, reporters can't seem to stop asking if there was any career rivalry between them. There isn't! "People are always like, 'Oh, are you afraid you're going to be in competition with your sister?'" Ashlee related to an interviewer. "I'm like, 'Hell no, I would rather be in competition with my sister than anybody else.' When two people in your family are out there doing it, it doesn't matter who wins because we're happy for each other."

In fact, in looking purely at album sales, Ashlee was actually the more successful recording artist in 2004. Her debut album, *Autobiography,* hit number one in its first week, while Jessica has never had an album reach number one, although her most recent CD, *In This Skin*, has sold a respectable 2.4 million copies in the United States.

Still, the Simpson girls are never competitive when it comes to album sales or business success. "We're sisters," Ashlee told the Associated Press. "For us, it's not about competition. If she succeeds, then I'm happy. And if I succeed, then our family wins no matter what."

"We're only competitive when it comes to who has the better outfit or gets more of Mom's time," Jessica confided to *People*. "She usually wins, 'cause she's the baby."

As for Ashlee, any lingering hurt feelings about having to live in the shadow of her sister's success for so long evaporated when *Autobiography* topped the charts. "It's different now because I'm actually [becoming successful] and it had nothing to do with her," Ashlee told the *Chicago Tribune*. "Jessica and I have actually switched, because she wants to go into acting. Now she comes to me for advice!"

All in the Family

Ashlee and Jessica Simpson have been the ones living in the spotlight, but they couldn't have gotten so far without the love and support of their parents, Joe and Tina Simpson, who have been with them every step of the way. From the very start, this couple from Texas encouraged their daughters to make their dreams come true.

As a stay-at-home mom, Tina was the driver who ferried her girls to everything from dance class to cheerleading practice to auditions. With a terrific eye for style, Tina also did most of the shopping for her daughters' wardrobes and acted as their style advisor. It a role she still enjoys to some extent today.

But, to answer the millions of TV viewers who wondered how Jessica could reach adulthood without knowing how to use a broom or why Ashlee has such trouble keeping track of her copious shoe collection — it's because selfless Tina did all the housework!

Though Joe didn't give up his job as a church minister and therapist right away, he has always been the guiding light of his daughters' careers. At first it wasn't easy because Joe, as a manager, lacked experience in the often underhanded world of big business. "[As a minister] I spent my time teaching people to tell the truth. So I was very big on my word," he explained. "And when it came to it, I assumed that if someone gave me their word, that was it. And boy, was I shocked. I kept saying, 'Wow, that's not what we talked about; that's not what we agreed on.' And it really screwed my mind up for a long time."

Fortunately, what Joe lacked in experience, he more than made up for in his willingness to dream big. "When it comes to the art of management and all the magical qualities it takes to be a great manager, Joe Simpson has them all," said Evan Lamberg, an EMI Music executive. "Trustworthy, honest, [with] great creative and business vision, [he is a] wonderful communicator, incredibly well organized and, maybe most importantly, he's beyond passionate about his artists and their music." Even P. Diddy is impressed with Joe's management — at the 2004 VMAs, Diddy gave Joe his business card and said, "Call me."

By brokering deals with MTV for his daughters' reality shows, Joe made Ashlee and Jessica more than just singers; he made them stars. "If you listen to what other people say, you'll never achieve your dreams," Joe told the *New York Times*. "I think I was desperate to help my children any way I could."

"We saw our children's talent and we were supportive of those talents," added Tina. "We gave up a lot so they could have their dreams come true."

Today, in addition to managing the careers of Jessica, Ashlee, Ryan Cabrera — and soon his son-in-law, Nick Lachey, if the rumors are true — Joe is the head of JT Records. The company, which was named for Joe and Tina, is helping new young acts get a foothold in the recording industry. Keep an eye out for Joe's newest discovery, five gorgeous guys in a group called Barefoot. Joe calls their music a cross between Third Eye Blind and veteran harmony group Crosby, Stills, Nash & Young.

"They're great kids," Joe enthused to *Billboard*. "I don't want to represent anyone who doesn't have a great heart. They aren't going to be divas; they're not full of themselves. They're nice. That's who JT Records is as far as artists go. I'm set on trying to bring that back to the business."

On a more personal note, Joe and Tina celebrated the creating of JT Records by purchasing a new $4-million home in Encino, California, not far from Jessica's estate and Ashlee's apartment. With six bedrooms, an outdoor pool with a waterfall, and their own basketball court and putting green, Joe and Tina can be assured to receive a lot of visits from the kids — and maybe grandkids!

But Joe hopes those grandkids don't arrive too soon. "I'm too young to be a grandfather!" Joe told a celebrity magazine. "In two years or so, hopefully Jessica will be in a place in her career where she can take off a year, have a baby, and then pick it back up again."

And who knows? If Jessica and Nick's babies can sing, there's no telling what a whole new generation can do with a little guidance from Joe!

CHAPTER 10
Meet Ryan Cabrera

A lot of his fans first discovered Dallas-born singer/ songwriter Ryan Cabrera when he appeared on *The Ashlee Simpson Show,* but this supertalented — and extremely hot — musician is a lot more than just Ashlee's "best friend." In fact, he was making huge strides in his music career long before he'd ever laid eyes on the lovely Ashlee.

Ryan was born on July 18, 1982, to Marc and Debbi Cabrera. Although he grew up hearing as much music as anybody, he didn't have any special love for it. He certainly didn't have any inkling that he'd grow up to become a musician. "I don't have a musical family, nobody sings or plays anything," he said on his official website.

But that all changed when a teenage Ryan discovered an old acoustic guitar at a friend's house

and started fooling around with it. "I started playing guitar kind of by accident and until that point I
never even thought about music," he confessed.
Although he wasn't good at it at first, the instru-
ment struck a chord with Ryan. He kept at it,
getting better and better at the guitar until he
knew enough actual chords to play a Beatles song.

Eventually, Ryan had mastered the guitar well
enough to want to play it in front of people. In high
school, he joined a punk band called Caine that
needed a guitarist. "The music was just as bad as
our name was," he remembered with a laugh.

Worse yet, Ryan's new bandmates wanted him
to sing! "I just wanted to play guitar, but it came
along with singing, I didn't really have a choice," he
said. "They just threw me up there. I'd never sung
in my life. I was horrible, of course."

A Different Direction

The course of Ryan's music made a U-turn when
he heard his first record by the Dave Matthews
Band. Singer/songwriter Dave Matthews, who's
been recording since 1994, opened up Ryan's eyes to
a more melodic brand of rock music. "I said, 'Okay,
this is going to be my life now,'" said Ryan. "I have

113

to start playing this music." Ryan left his band Caine and eventually created another one, Rubic's Groove, which was more in line with his newfound love of deeper lyrics and hummable melodies.

Before Ryan even graduated from high school, Rubic's Groove developed a following around Dallas, becoming the city's most popular live act. Flush with his new success, Ryan was thrilled to be invited to share concert bills with veteran bands like Cheap Trick and hot alt-radio staples like Ben Harper and Third Eye Blind. After graduation, Ryan enrolled in the University of Texas along with the rest of his bandmates. Rubic's Groove soon became the hottest band on campus.

As a birthday present, Ryan's older brother bought him a block of time at a local Dallas recording studio, Deep Ellum Studios. "I went in there, just by myself, and I did three songs I had written. And it went really, really well," Ryan recalls.

In fact, Ryan sounded so good that an engineer at Deep Ellum offered to record an album of Ryan's music for free. Though Ryan felt bad about leaving the rest of his bandmates in Rubic's Groove behind, he couldn't resist what seemed like a too-good-to-be-true offer.

"I had never really thought of playing solo, or

ever doing anything like that," he explained. "I was in a band."

But Ryan ended up recording a collection of songs he's been writing over the past two years. His indie album, *Elm Street*, was released in 2001 and soon became popular on college radio stations. Buoyed by his success, Ryan became a solo act permanently.

But that wasn't the only big change in his life. "When my parents went out of town, I quit school," he explained on his official website. "Oh yeah, they were angry. They flipped. I quit school because I really wanted to concentrate on singing, because I was really never a singer-singer. I really didn't know what I was doing."

After he left school, Ryan started working full-time with a vocal coach in Dallas who was intent on teaching him how to make the most of his voice. It wasn't easy. "She taught me a bunch of exercises to do which were really insane, unheard-of things," Ryan recalled. "We would do 1,200 'bicycles' a day, which are kind of like ab-crunches. I also had to lift up chairs and hold them while I was singing scales. Both of these are diaphragm exercises. It was like torture, but it really helped."

In the same way that Ryan had become

obsessed with learning the guitar, he suddenly poured all his energy into becoming the best singer he could be — to the exclusion of everything else in his life. "For five months, I sat in my room and sang four or five hours a day," he said. "I sang scales and held up chairs and did stuff in military positions, all these crazy exercises. I didn't really see anybody. I woke up, sang, and went to bed. Five months. And then after that I felt ready."

While on tour opening a string of dates for Australian songwriter and guitarist Howie Day, Ryan met Joe Simpson, Ashlee and Jessica's manager and dad, who signed him up as the first client who wasn't a daughter. Still, Joe couldn't help making Ryan part of the family. "He's like my son. I love him," Joe said of Ryan. "I signed him after I heard him the first time in Dallas."

Ryan began working on his major-label debut album for Atlantic Records in early 2004 in Los Angeles.

To help him learn the craft of songwriting, his label set Ryan up with a string of veteran songwriters. "I wrote every single day, most of the time with someone new, so it was insane," recalls Ryan. "I ended up spending three months [in Los Angeles]. That's where I met John."

John Rzeznik is the lead singer of the Goo Goo Dolls, whose hits include "Iris" and "Slide." The Grammy-winning songwriter and Ryan hit it off so well that when it came time for Atlantic Records and Ryan to choose a producer, John offered himself up for the position.

"John said, 'I've never produced anything before, but I could do this, *we* could do this,'" recalls Ryan. John and Ryan became coproducers. "We went into the recording studio a week and a half later and we recorded the whole record in a month," recalled Ryan. "John had to go on tour, so we were under the gun."

Though it wasn't always smooth sailing, recording *Take It All Away* drew Ryan and John closer together. "We were like brothers, to the point where we looked out for each other, we fought," Ryan told MTV. "We loved each other, we hated each other. We went through it all."

Ryan's album *Take It All Away* was released on August 17, 2004 and hit the number eight spot on the *Billboard* album charts. It certainly didn't hurt that its first single, the sunny but rocking "On the Way Down," was featured prominently in the third episode of *The Ashlee Simpson Show*.

But while many fans might think that "On the

Way Down" is about Ashlee, Ryan said that it's not. He actually wrote the first draft of the song two years before he'd ever met her. "'On the Way Down' is a spiritual song about being saved," Ryan told Alloy. The song was based on his personal experience of wanting more than his life was offering. "I had everything going: great family, money, good school . . . but I was missing something," he said. "Everyone needs something to pull them out of that — a girl, a dude, a dog — whatever. So I left that song open to interpretation."

Best Friends

Ashlee came into Ryan's life unexpectedly, but long before they became a romantic duo they were the best of pals. "My voice teacher [in Dallas] asked me if I wanted to take her out," Ryan remembered in an interview. "She was like, 'Ashlee's coming into town for some lessons. She doesn't know too many people here. Do you want to take her out?' She came in and made me sing for her the first time I met her."

Despite the fix-up, no real sparks flew between Ryan and Ashlee immediately, which is probably okay because Ryan ended up living with the Simpson family as he recorded his album in Los

Angeles. "He's like my son," Joe Simpson told a celebrity magazine. "He lived with us for six months. He and Ashlee were best friends. At the time, Ryan was dating Ashlee's best friend from the time she was three."

"We were like brother and sister," added Ryan. "We lived next door to each other, room to room. But she was dating Josh — until my music video."

Making Ashlee the love interest in Ryan's video wasn't either singer's idea — that stroke of genius came from Joe Simpson. "I didn't know I was setting up a romance!" he told a reporter. "I asked Ryan to put Ashlee as the love interest in his video because I thought it would be a great moment for the video because people know Ashlee."

Fans of *The Ashlee Simpson Show* saw the rapid change in their relationship on the set of the video shoot. One minute they were buddies, kidding around. In the next, Ashlee was pinning Ryan up against a wall for a lingering kiss.

Even today, Ashlee has a hard time putting into words exactly what made her suddenly look at Ryan as more than just a buddy. "He has been my best friend for a long time," she told an interviewer. "And I was the girl in his video. Something just happened. We hit it off and we had our first kiss in that

119

and from then on, I don't know what happened. . . . We had been friends for so long and it kind of just clicked."

Ashlee tried to sum it up better in another interview: "I had a BF, and he had a GF, and we were, like, totally not interested in each other. We were just best friends, and then I don't know what happened. We just sorta started liking each other."

Even if Ashlee can't pinpoint what changed her feelings for Ryan at that moment, she can certainly explain why he's so special to her today. "I like people who are comfortable in their skin," she told Alloy. "I think the most attractive thing is a sense of humor. Somebody that makes jokes — bad jokes, funny jokes, awkward, and weird jokes too! Just somebody who doesn't take him- or herself so dang seriously."

Ryan, with his highly evolved sense of humor, totally filled the bill. "Ryan is absolutely hysterical," she explains. "That's why I have so much fun with him. He is just so funny. I come home so stressed, and he totally just makes everything okay."

Joe Simpson also approves of Ryan. "He's a great kid," Joe told a reporter. "He's got a wonderful heart."

For his part, Ryan is very happy to have Ashlee in his life — whether she's just his buddy or something more. "She's the most unique girl I've ever met. There's no other Ashlee in the world," he said. "I like someone who's really relaxed and comfortable — a girl that doesn't take herself too seriously. If a girl can have fun and be herself, then I love that."

Ryan adds: "Talk about the epitome of not caring about anything — that's delicious Ash."

When discussing the future of their relationship, this on-again, off-again couple is also perfectly in tune. "Right now, we're both concentrating on our careers," Ryan said. "That's the first thing. We love spending time together, so when we get a chance, we do. But that's why we've been on and off, because it's hard when she's on the road or I'm on the road."

"It's just fun," added Ashlee about their relationship. "I love everything that I'm doing right now. I'm having so much fun [with] my first album. I want to enjoy all that and not be worried about a guy. We both like each other — a lot. But labels scare me right now."

Ryan's Future

Whether Ryan and Ashlee's love will stand the test of time is a mystery, but there is no doubt that their friendship, and both of their careers, will continue to thrive. Like Ashlee, Ryan has had a terrific time playing his music live. He spent most of 2004 on the road: first as the opening act for Jessica, then on his own college tour, a mall tour, and finally with Ashlee for a couple of high school dates.

On his tour of colleges, flirtatious Ryan had a blast knocking on the door of sorority houses in hope of convincing the sorority sisters to come out and see his show. "I sat like 40 or 50 girls down in the living room and I would sing them one song," he explained to MTV. "And they'd be like, 'Sing another one!' I'd be like, 'No, you've got to come to the show.' And then I would leave."

Clearly, Ryan already has enough charm to be the Pied Piper, but he says that his long-term goals go way beyond just enticing the girls. He plans to become a better songwriter and a more dynamic live performer.

For songwriting inspiration, he looks to veteran singer/songwriters like Paul Simon and Van Morrison. "I have to be that good," he said. "The same feeling that they create for me, I have to do for someone else. I still have a long way to go, but I know what I have to do to get better. I'm going to do whatever it takes to be able to affect people the same way I've been affected by the music I love."

Ryan also wants his live shows to be exciting experiences that audience members will remember long after the house lights are switched on. "I play guitar. I write my songs. I want to play longer," he explained to MTV. "I don't want to be somebody who just comes in and goes out. I want people to see that I can actually play.

"I want to do this forever," he adds, "not just a couple of records."

CHAPTER 11
Did You Know?

1. Ashlee Nicole Simpson was born on October 3, 1984, in Dallas, Texas.

2. One of Ashlee's favorite singers is sixties rocker Janis Joplin. "Her soul-rock is amazing," Ashlee told the *New York Times*.

3. Though Ashlee admires the music of often-troubled rocker Courtney Love, she could never live with that much drama in her own life! "That life is too much," opined Ashlee to the *New York Times*. "Oh God, I couldn't imagine it. But some people, that's just who they are."

4. Ashlee would love to see more girls get into rock music. "I love Pat Benatar, Stevie Nicks,

Deborah Harry, Chrissie Hynde, these women who were sexy and rocked and they just had this strong characteristic about them," she told MTV. "Tough girls. I like that. They had something to say, and I like it when people really do speak truly, and I hope people hear that in my record."

5. Watching *The Ashlee Simpson Show* has been fun for its star — even if she had to live through her tough breakup with Josh again. "It's interesting to watch, but fun," she said during an MSN chat. "Me and my friends watch it together and we always get a kick out of it."

6. Ashlee doesn't remember the first CD she ever bought, but she does remember listening to Van Halen, a favorite of one of her cousins, at age four!

7. Ashlee says her favorite bands are Jimmy Eat World, the Pretenders, and Maroon 5.

8. One of Ashlee's favorite places to shop is Urban Outfitters. She's also a fan of designer Marc

125

Jacobs and loves to dig through the racks at vintage clothing shops.

9. Ashlee enjoys acting, but she loves singing most. "Even though playing characters is really fun, when you're a singer you get to be you," she said during an MSN chat.

10. Ashlee admits she was starstruck to meet actress Ashley Judd, but unfortunately, the meeting didn't go well. "I was 13 and I went up to her and she wouldn't say hi," Ashlee recalled during an MSN chat. "She probably was not in the mood. I was so sad. I just wanted to tell her that I was a younger sister too but she wouldn't look at me."

11. Ashlee's favorite songs on her album are "Nothing New" and "Undiscovered."

12. Ashlee has a bracelet that was a gift from her sister. It's inscribed with the words: "If you can dream it, you can be it."

13. Ashlee's favorite movie is the R-rated *True*

Romance. "It's violent, but the love story is good," she said during an MSN chat.

14. Ashlee's favorite candies are Laughy Taffy and Nerds.

15. Her favorite footwear is high heels by designer Stella McCartney and Marc Jacobs boots.

16. Like Jessica, Ashlee is a bit messy! Her clothes and cosmetics overflow their drawers in her bedroom and bathroom.

17. Ashlee's a pretty good cook. "I'm good at making tacos," she told *US*.

18. Her apartment has two vending machines — one in the kitchen and one in her recording studio — that serve ice-cold cans of Red Bull.

19. Ashlee would love to jam with another MTV reality star: Ozzy Osbourne. "He's got the most amazing voice," she told an interviewer. "I always wonder how he can be so, like, crazy and

out of it and then he gets up on the mic and he's just unbelievable."

20. Ashlee has sensitive skin, so she only cleanses her face with Cetaphil cleanser. And she always remembers to wash the makeup off her face before she goes to bed each night no matter how tired she is.

21. Ashlee also tries to do sit-ups every night before going to sleep.

22. She doesn't follow a specific diet. "I allow myself to eat whatever I want," she told a reporter. "But I try to eat in moderation."

23. Her sometimes-boyfriend Ryan Cabrera was there for support when Ashlee shot the photos for her Candies print advertisement.

24. Ashlee says that now that she has dark hair, her appearance is often compared with the Pretenders singer, Chrissie Hynde. "I consider that a huge compliment," she told a reporter. "When I first wore my hair like this I

thought, 'Oh God, I look like an eighties rocker chic!'"

25. Ashlee originally didn't want to do an MTV reality show. "The real reason I decided to do the TV show is I wanted people to see the separation from my sister," Ashlee told the *Los Angeles Times*. "We're completely different."

26. Ashlee shares her birth date, October 3, with No Doubt singer Gwen Stefani. The two rock chicks met each other for the first time at the 2004 Video Music Awards. "She's so rad!" said Ashlee.

27. Ashlee's favorite vacation spot is Cabo San Lucas. "It makes you feel like you are really somewhere else."

28. For her sister's 24th birthday, Ashlee bought Jessica a big Louis Vuitton suitcase. "I never know what to get her because she has everything," Ashlee complained.

29. Ashlee would love to have a dog. "I just don't

think I could take care of one now because my life is so crazy," she says.

30. As an adolescent, Ashlee used to like to lock the door of her bedroom, sprawl across the bed, and write about what she was feeling.

31. Before Ryan Cabrera dated Ashlee, he was romantically involved with her best friend from Texas!

32. When Ashlee was in London performing on *Top of the Pops*, she became pals with Danni Minogue, a singer who's also the younger sister to an international hit-maker, Kylie Minogue. The two little sisters had so much in common that Danni promised Ashlee that the next time she's in London, Danni will fix her up with a cute guy!

33. Ashlee was glad that she and Josh broke up after she watched episodes of *The Ashlee Simpson Show*. "Watching it just make me realize how idiotic he was," she told a reporter.

34. After Ashlee and Ryan broke up, they promised

they'd still be friends and to even go on dates with each other when they were in the same place.

35. Both Jessica and Ashlee use celebrity hairstylist Ken Paves to style their fabulous locks. Shhhh! To make Ashlee's brunette hair look fuller, he gave her hair extensions.

37. Ashlee and Jessica can both burp on command!

38. She would love to record a song with her sometime boyfriend. "Ryan is so talented," she said. "He's an amazing guitar player and an amazing writer, and I would *love* to do something with him."

39. Jessica and Ashlee say they've never had a real fight. "No, it's always stupid stuff," said Jessica. "Like if she takes all my makeup and all my clothes."

40. The Simpson sisters are such complete opposites that they can look at the same clothes and want to wear them differently. "We can look at the same outfit and I'll rip the shirt up and do

all that kind of stuff, where she's very glam," Ashlee told MTV.

41. Ashlee hasn't ruled out recording another song with Jessica someday. "I'd like to do something different for the both of us," Ashlee told the Associated Press. "Maybe blues or something where we can both step out of our styles."

42. Ashlee is willing to try anything. "You have one life to live. Why not have turquoise hair for two months of it?" she told *People*.

43. Like her talented daughters, Tina Simpson has a good voice. "Me, her, and Jessica sing together all the time," Ashlee told the *New York Times*. "We'll sing, like, gospel songs or, whatever, blues songs."

44. If Ashlee had to choose one word to describe herself it would be impulsive. "I love to do things by the minute," she said. "If it's to dye my hair brown — whatever it is — I just like to kind of go for it and put myself out there, and do fun stuff. I'm very random!"

45. Some of Ashlee's favorite pastimes are watching movies at home with her girlfriends, bowling, and going out dancing.

46. What's a perfect date for Ashlee? "I think it would be fun to go to the zoo," she told Alloy. "I know it's really weird and random, but I just think it would be a lot of fun. I love animals, and I think it'd be like a day of doing silly things, while enjoying nature."

47. Ashlee's dream date would be going out with Adam Levine and Ryan Dusick, the singer and drummer, from Maroon 5. She thinks they're both really hot and has a hard time choosing between them.

48. Ryan took Ashlee to a John Mayer concert before John was huge. She didn't like John then, but Ashlee loves his music now. "Ryan always introduces me to new stuff," she said.

49. Ashlee drives a Lexus convertible sedan. It's black with a tan interior.

50. Want to say hi to Ashlee? Her official website is ashleesimpsonmusic.com.

Ashlee Gets the Last Word

A few notable quotables from Ashlee's many interviews!

"I'm going through some defining moments in my life. I've tried not to hold anything back."

"I love to be a dork with my friends and have fun."

"I feel like I have my own identity and I stand on my own."

"With singing, you're letting your guard down and opening yourself up in front of people; it's the real you."

"I'm a tomboy with a girly twist."

"I love you, and love my life, and thank you for letting me be myself."

"I work my butt off . . . I wouldn't do it if I didn't love the music."

"I'm so excited for what's happened and what's to come. I am so thankful for everyone's support."

Ashlee Simpson's Autobiography

1. Autobiography
2. Pieces of Me
3. Shadow
4. La La
5. Love Makes the World Go Round
6. Better Off
7. Love Me for Me
8. Surrender
9. Unreachable
10. Nothing New
11. Giving It All Away
12. Undiscovered

Photo Credits